Seasonal
PRESERVES

Seasonal
PRESERVES

Joanna Farrow

NEW
HOLLAND

First published in 2010
by New Holland Publishers (UK) Ltd
London • Cape Town • Sydney • Auckland

Garfield House
86–88 Edgware Rd
London W2 2EA
United Kingdom

80 McKenzie Street
Cape Town 8001
South Africa

Unit 1
66 Gibbes Street
Chatswood
NSW 2067
Australia

218 Lake Road
Northcote
Auckland
New Zealand

ISBN 978 1 84773 438 9

Publisher: Clare Sayer
Senior Editor: Emma Pattison
Cover Design: Fiona Andreanelli
Layout Design: Beverly Price, www.one2six.com
Food Photography: Sue Atkinson and Ian Garlick
Food Stylist: Joanna Farrow
Props Stylist: Roisin Nield
Senior Production Controller: Marion Stortz
Editorial Direction: Rosemary Wilkinson

10 9 8 7 6 5 4 3 2 1

Reproduction by Pica Digital Pte Ltd, Singapore
Printed and bound in Malaysia by Times Offset (M)
Sdn Bhd

Contents

Introduction

As a form of cooking, preserving is so unlike any other. Instead of labouring in the kitchen to provide regular meals – which are gone in ten minutes – preserving has quite the opposite outcome. Jars, pots and bottles are filled with tempting treats that will last right through the year, providing a feast of flavours for topping toast, filling cakes, spooning over snacks or simply dipping into whenever you get the urge. This is why preserving is one of my favourite forms of cooking and something I never tire of. I also love using seasonal produce, both from the garden and those I buy when at their best, so I can be sure of their good provenance and therefore good results! Even better is the fun of foraging for free food. Gathering elderflower heads for cordial and brambles for jelly are two of my therapeutic seasonal rituals. Making preserves has a reputation for being at the least slightly tricky and time consuming, but this isn't the case. Boiling up fruit with sugar to make jam is really not difficult, and throwing a selection of vegetables into a pan for chutney is about as simple as it gets. The recipes in this book provide a selection of both classic and more innovative recipes for jams, jellies, marmalades, chutneys and other less obvious preserves. Generally, they make manageable quantities too. No one, after all, wants to live on the same flavour marmalade for years! If you do get carried away on the preserve trail, share them out or give as presents. Any foodie friend would no doubt prefer a personalized, designer-potted preserve to a mass-produced box of chocolates.

types of preserves

The seasonal recipes you will find on the following pages include the classic preserves, such as jams and chutneys, as well as some more unusual oils, vinegars and fruits in syrup.

jams The jams in this book range from the classic favourite *Strawberry* (page 50) to the less conventional *Spiced Rhubarb and Apple* (page 21) and *Blueberry and Vanilla* (page 49). Mid- to late summer is traditional jam-making season and the aroma of soft summer fruits, bubbling away in their syrupy juices, is certainly one of the best. Conserves are a type of jam in which larger pieces of fruit are suspended in a sweet syrup. They don't set as firmly as jams, and their syrupy juices will no doubt run all over the plate of whatever they're accompanying. Use them more as a fabulous topping for ice cream, sponge cakes or creamy yogurt.

jellies Of all the homemade preserves, it's the jellies that I find most absorbing to make, possibly due to their gorgeous colours, which range from the palest pastels to deep burgundy reds. Some cooks might be put off making jellies because of the need to strain them for several hours (or overnight if made late in the day), but straining really is so easy if you use the simple method on page 10. Even easier is the fact that there's so little fruit preparation beforehand; cores, stalks, skins, pips and stones are all thrown in the pan for the initial cooking and only larger fruits need a rough chopping first.

marmalades Marmalades generally require a bit more preparation than other preserves. Cut the shreds as finely or as thickly as you prefer – using a food processor is a quick and easy way of finely chopping the peel if you don't like a proper 'shredded' marmalade. One watchpoint is the consistency of the cooked peel before adding any sugar. A piece of softened peel, lifted from the pan, should be soft and fall apart between your fingers. Once the sugar is added the peel won't soften any more and the cooked shreds will have a hard, chewy texture.

fruit curds and cheeses A tangy fruit curd is another preserve that can readily be bought but simply doesn't have the vibrant flavour of a homemade one. Fruit 'cheeses' bear no relation to dairy produce but are instead, a preserve made by cooking fresh fruits to a thick, pulpy paste. Sweetened and flavoured with spices, or simply left plain, they make a great addition to the cheeseboard in a similar vane to Membrillo, the Spanish quince cheese served with tapas. Fruit 'butters' have a softer consistency than fruit cheeses and are served as you would jam.

chutneys and relishes
Chutneys and relishes can be made at any time of year, but the abundant supplies of fruit and vegetables in late summer makes this the most practical time for potting up supplies to take you through the winter. Most chutneys are best left for a couple of weeks before use to let their flavours mingle and mellow and from then on will keep well, and taste good, almost until you're ready to make the next batch. Relishes are made in a similar way but are not cooked to such a pulpy consistency. Fresh tasting and with a crunchier texture, they have a shorter storage time of up to four months.

pickles
Like chutneys, pickles have a high vinegar content, which needs to mellow for several weeks before use or the flavour can be a bit harsh. Vegetable pickles such as *Cucumber, Dill and Mustard* (page 74) are great with a slice of chunky bread and wedge of cheese, or smoked fish or cold meats. Sweet pickled fruits such as *Vanilla Pickled Plums* (page 113) or *Saffron Pickled Pears* (page 114) are lovely, chopped and scattered over salads, their sweet syrupy juices added to dressings and sauces.

sauces, oils, vinegars and seasonings
The recipes here are a selection of ideas from savoury sauces to preserved vegetables, mustard and homemade cheese, giving a little taster of the vast scope of preserves that can be made, effortlessly and absorbingly, at home.

mincemeat and fruits in syrup
Bottling fruits in syrup is such a great way of extending the relatively short season of some of our favourite fruits, and guarantees a supply of effortless desserts for months ahead. For casual suppers, present the fruits in their jars for spooning over whipped or clotted cream, mascarpone, vanilla ice cream and maybe some dessert biscuits to add crunch and texture. Mincemeats are just about the easiest preserve of all and the two in this book are really special. They store well but should be checked occasionally. If the surface dries out, top up with a dash of liqueur or, if they start to ooze syrup, boil up in a pan, re-pot and store in the fridge.

cordials and drinks
There's such satisfaction in serving homemade cordials, their freshness and purity of flavour vastly superior to most bought ones. The trickiest part is keeping up with nature's supplies – elderflowers (briefly) in early summer and brambles in the autumn. Think ahead when making alcoholic drinks as they need several months to mellow and mature.

equipment

I've made many of the recipes in this book with little more than a
saucepan, scales, chopping board, knife and a few saved jam jars,
which illustrates just how simple preserve making can be.

preserving pan A good-quality preserving pan is deep and wide, designed
for 'boiling up' jams, jellies and marmalades without the risk of the mixture boiling
over the top. Their solid, 'heavy base' means you can cook pulpy, thick sauces and
chutneys without running the risk of the mixture sticking to the base of the pan.
They're available in stainless steel, lined aluminium or copper, and enamel and have
a carrying handle as well as a side handle for tipping the pan to ladle out the last of
the preserve for potting. Don't fill the preserving pan (or saucepan) more than half
full so there's plenty of space for the preserve to rise up as it boils. Some preserves
need covering with a lid during the early stages of cooking. If your preserving pan
doesn't have a lid, improvise by using a large baking sheet or sheet of foil, secured
around the edges of the pan. If you're not sure about how much use you'll get from
a preserving pan, bear in mind that they're also good for large-scale catering, i.e.
soup for a crowd, and they also make a great stockpot.

sugar thermometers Jams, jellies and marmalades need to be boiled for
a certain amount of time before potting. A sugar thermometer isn't essential, but
it'll give you an idea of when the preserve is nearly ready. Clip the thermometer to
the side of the pan when you start to boil the preserve and boil until the
temperature reaches 105°C (221°F). At that point, test for a set (see page 13).

long-handled wooden spoons These are useful when making large
quantities of preserves, ensuring that your fingers don't get too close to the hot
liquid when stirring.

slotted or perforated spoons These are used for skimming off the
layer of scum that sometimes forms when boiling jams, jellies and marmalades. Use
a long-handled one with small holes or thin slots. If the slots are too big the spoon
won't skim efficiently.

jelly bags Made from cotton or nylon mesh, jelly bags are used for straining
the juice from fruit pulp when making jellies. They can be suspended from a
kitchen cupboard door over a bowl to catch the juice or can be bought with a stand
so they can be left on the work surface. A simple alternative (and one I used
throughout the book) is to line a large bowl with muslin so it overhangs the edges,
pour in the fruit and pulp, gather the edges up over the pulp and secure in a bundle
with string to suspend. Don't press the pulp through the bag to speed up the
process or the jelly will be cloudy.

preserving funnels These help keep things tidy when potting preserves into jars. Rest the funnel over each jar as you fill it and the mixture won't spill out down the sides of the jar.

jam jars Any heatproof glass jars can be used for preserves. Recycle your own empty jam, chutney, marmalade, olive or sauce jars (it's amazing how quickly you can build up a collection). If making for presents you might want to buy more interestingly shaped 'designer' jars. Have the cleaned and sterilized jars ready and waiting to take the hot preserve. If you're oven sterilizing them, leave them in there until the preserve is ready. If you've used the dishwasher to sterilize them and the cycle has finished before the preserve is ready, they'll be fine if you leave them there for a while with the door closed.

sterilizing jars Wash new or used jars in warm, soapy water, discarding any old labels. Sometimes these come off easily if left to soak in the water for a while. If not, use a scourer to scrape off the labels and stubborn glue. (Liquid lighter fuel or commercial 'sticky-label remover' is useful for glue that simply won't rub off). Once clean and dry, put the jars on a kitchen-paper-lined baking sheet in the oven at 150°C/300°F/Gas Mark 2, for at least 15 minutes. Most preserves are potted while still hot so leave the jars in the oven if the preserve isn't quite ready. An alternative sterilizing method is to use the regular dishwasher cycle.

bottles and other preserving jars Narrow screw-topped or clip-topped bottles can be used for sauces and cordials while wide-necked ones are good for bottled fruits or pickles. Kilner and Le Parfait are two of the most widely available, but other brands can be used as long as they're suitable for preserves. Jams, chutneys and marmalades also look good in clip-topped jars.

jam pot covers Packs of jam pot covers, available in 450–900 g (1–2 lb) sizes are used for sealing jams, jellies and marmalades. The waxed discs are pressed gently onto the surface of the jam, before covering with cellophane. Drizzle the top of a cellophane disc with cold water before pulling it taut over the jar and securing with elastic.

preserving plungers Whole pieces of fruit or vegetables have a tendency to rise to the top of jars once potted. Plastic preserving 'plungers' can be placed on top of the preserve to keep the ingredients submerged in the liquid.

techniques

Preserve making is so rewarding that you're bound to get hooked! Here's a few essential techniques to get you started and you'll soon be well on your way to making delicious preserves for friends and family.

making jams, jellies and marmalades
Jams, jellies and marmalades share several similar techniques, i.e. softening of fruits, boiling with sugar and testing for a set. Use fruits that are only just ripe, rather than over-ripe and cut out any blemishes or damaged parts. Generally, fruits don't need washing first as they're cooked at such high temperatures. Where possible use unwaxed or organic citrus fruits, particularly if the zest is to be used in the recipe.

pectin
Pectin, a gum-like substance found in varying levels in fruits, is what makes a preserve set. Slightly under-ripe fruit contains more pectin than over-ripe ones, and different fruits vary in their pectin levels (see below). Those high in pectin such as apples and cranberries will set easily, while those with a low pectin content are more difficult to set. To make setting easier, combine a low-pectin fruit such as rhubarb with apples, which will almost guarantee a good set. Alternatively, add plenty of lemon juice to a low-pectin fruit such as strawberries, as the pectin reacts with acids to make a good set. If it still doesn't set, don't boil the jam indefinitely – better a lightly set jam (which is still delicious) than one that almost turned to caramel and lost its fresh fruity flavour! Another way of setting low-pectin fruits is to use 'jam sugar', which has added pectin.

testing for pectin content
A simple way of testing the pectin level of the fruit is to put a teaspoonful of the cooked fruit pulp (before you've added the sugar) into a small dish and cool. Add 1 tablespoon methylated spirit and swirl lightly together before tipping out onto a plate. If the fruit has a slightly jelly-like consistency, there is sufficient pectin. If still liquid, you'll need to add more pectin to get a reasonable set.

Pectin Levels of Fruits

High	cooking apples, crab apples, cranberries, citrus fruits, damsons, gooseberries, redcurrants, blackcurrants, plums (some types), quinces
Medium	apricots, blackberries, dessert apples, greengages, loganberries, mulberries, raspberries, plums
Low	bananas, cherries, figs, grapes, melons, nectarines, peaches, pears, pineapples, rhubarb, strawberries

warming the sugar This isn't essential when making jams, jellies and marmalades, but can help to speed up the sugar dissolving and sugar boiling process, therefore maintaining the fresh flavours of the fruits. Put the sugar in a large, ovenproof bowl and heat through in a moderate oven, 160°C/325°F/Gas Mark 3 for about 15 minutes before tipping into the pan.

testing for a set Once the sugar has dissolved into the fruit juice and the mixture is brought to a rapid boil, a set should be reached between 5 and 20 minutes, depending on the fruit used. There are several ways of testing whether it's ready.

saucer test Put a spoonful of the mixture onto a chilled saucer or plate and put in the fridge for a couple of minutes. (Turn off the heat while you do so.) Push your finger through the cooled mixture. If the surface wrinkles, it's ready, if not, reboil for a few more minutes and try again.

flake test Lift a little of the preserve from the pan and let it cool a little. Tilt the spoon so the syrup drops back into the pan. If the preserve is ready, the syrup will clot together and break cleanly off the spoon. If it runs off the spoon, reboil for a few minutes and try again.

temperature test Clip a sugar thermometer to the side of the pan once the sugar is dissolved. The jam is ready when the temperature registers 105°C (221°F) on the thermometer. To be absolutely sure, check by doing the flake or saucer tests.

potting Unless otherwise stated in a recipe, preserves are potted while still hot. If you're making one that contains chunky pieces of fruit, such as *Pineapple and Stem Ginger Conserve* on page 21, let the preserve stand for 15 minutes, then lightly stir before potting. This helps to suspend the fruit in the fruity syrup so that it doesn't all rise to the surface once potted. Cover with waxed discs and jam pot covers while still hot. Metal, screw-topped lids can be used instead of the cellophane ones.

making chutneys and relishes
Chutneys and relishes are probably the easiest preserves to make as all the ingredients are cooked in the pan together and there's no 'testing for a set' to worry about. All you need to do is give the mixture the occasional stir, until it reaches that pulpy, chutney-like consistency.

checking consistency
Most of the chutneys in this book take between 30 minutes and 1 hour to cook. Because the liquid needs to evaporate as the chutney cooks, don't cover the pan with a lid. Stir the mixture frequently using a long-handled spoon (as the mixture might splutter slightly as it thickens). The chutney is ready when the spoon is drawn across the base of the pan, briefly leaving a clear channel, which gradually fills up with juices.

filling jars
Pack the chutney into thoroughly clean, warm jars. Because chutneys and relishes contain a high proportion of vinegar, which acts as a preservative, sterilizing the jars isn't essential, though it's just as easy to have them ready and waiting in the oven.

covering jars
Don't use jam pot covers on chutneys and relishes as, over time, the vinegar will evaporate through the covers. Instead use clip-top preserving jars or ordinary jars with plastic-lined, screw-topped lids.

brining pickles
There are two basic ways of preparing vegetables for pickling. The first is 'wet brining' in which the whole or cut vegetables are immersed in salt and water. This is used mainly for firm-textured vegetables such as onions or shallots. Vegetables containing a higher water content are 'dry brined'. For this, the whole or chopped vegetables are layered up in a bowl with plenty of salt, which extracts the excess water from the vegetables before pickling. After dry brining, make sure you thoroughly rinse the vegetables in several changes of cold water to remove all traces of salt.

oven sterilizing

Some of the fruits in syrup in the recipe chapters are sterilized in the oven, once potted, to extend their storage time. (The same preserves, if not oven-sterilized, can be made and stored in the fridge for several weeks.) For fruit recipes, such as *Honeyed Apricots* (page 49), use wide-necked preserving jars, either with rubber seals and clip-on lids, or metal screw-topped jars. Sterilize the empty jars as on page 11 and fill, following recipe instructions. Loosely screw on the lids or position clip lids without fastening them down. Arrange jars in a newspaper-lined roasting tin, spaced slightly apart. Cook in the oven, preheated to 150°C/300°F/Gas Mark 2 for the time stated in the recipe. Turn off the oven and leave to cool slightly before lifting from the oven and sealing the lids firmly.

testing the seal

Once the jars are completely cold, test the seal to make sure a vacuum has formed. Remove clips or screw bands and carefully lift the jars by their lids. If it remains attached a vacuum has formed and the preserve will store successfully. If not, store the preserve in the fridge and use within two weeks.

sterilizing sauces

Sauces can be bottled and preserved by heating them using a slow water bath in a saucepan. (The preserves, if not sterilized, can be made and stored in the fridge for several weeks.) Use bottles with either screw-topped lids or rubber, clip-on stoppers. Sterilize the empty bottles and fill to 2 cm (¾ in) of the rims with sauce. Loosely screw on screw tops or position rubber, clip-on stoppers without securing the clips. Line a deep saucepan with a trivet or thicknesses of newspaper and place bottles slightly apart. Fill the pan with warm water to the base of the caps and slowly bring to a simmer. Clip a thermometer to the side of the pan if you have one. It should register 77°C (170°F). Heat for 30 minutes then turn off the heat and ladle out a little water. Using oven gloves, lift out bottles and leave to cool.

storing preserves The preserves in this book have varying storage times, from short term to those that'll keep for up to a year. The storage times given should be used as a guide as they vary slightly depending on the environment. Check the preserves occasionally. All unrefrigerated preserves will keep best if kept in a cool cupboard (away from the kitchen if necessary), which must also be dark and dry. A damp environment will encourage mould formation on the preserves.

Spring

Whether you're a home grower, or have to rely on markets or supermarkets, the spring is a fairly sparse time for fresh home-grown produce. Instead, we can rely on fruit and vegetables that enjoy all year abundance such as onions, cabbages, grapes, pineapples and other tropical fruits. The delicate stalks of forced rhubarb are now in good supply and are one of early spring's favourite and best offerings. In the garden, it's usually the herbs that are the first plants to flourish. Young, tender and packed with flavour they're great for flavouring oils and vinegars, as well as aromatic salt, which provides a great 'season all' for your cooking over the months ahead. A fresh batch can be made later in the summer. The spring is also a good time for making citrusy drinks and smooth buttery curds, both making great gifts for friends and family.

spiced rhubarb and apple jam

The first new season rhubarb, known as 'forced rhubarb', is grown under cover. The pastel, rose-tinted, tender stalks are perfect for preserving, unlike the coarser 'outdoor' rhubarb that comes into season in early summer. This soft-textured jam is mildly spiced with ginger and cloves to complement the flavour of both fruits. Put the cloves in with the trimmings in the muslin bag if you don't want the whole pieces in the finished jam.

makes 2.4 kg (5¼ lb)   **preparation time** 30 mins   **cooking time** 35 mins

1 kg (2 lb 3 oz) cooking apples, peeled, cored and roughly chopped, reserving the peel and cores

Finely grated zest and juice of 2 lemons

820 g (1 lb 13 oz) young tender rhubarb, trimmed and cut into 2 cm (¾ in) lengths

25 g (1 oz) fresh root ginger, chopped

2 tsp whole cloves

1.5 kg (3 lb 5 oz) preserving or granulated sugar

Put the chopped apples in a preserving pan or large saucepan. Add the lemon zest and juice and 600 ml (1 pint) water. Tie the reserved apple peel, cores and lemon pips in a large square of muslin and add to the pan.

Bring to the boil, reduce the heat, cover and simmer gently for 5 minutes. Add the rhubarb and return to the boil. Reduce the heat again, cover and simmer for a further 8–10 minutes until the rhubarb is tender but still retaining a little shape.

Remove the muslin bag, squeezing it against the side of the pan to extract all the juices. Stir in the ginger, cloves and sugar and heat gently, stirring, until the sugar dissolves.

Bring to the boil and boil until setting point is reached, skimming any scum from the surface. This will take about 15–20 minutes.

Ladle into sterilized jars, cover and label.

pineapple and stem ginger conserve

This preserve can be made at any time of year, but is perhaps a good one to make in spring when home-grown fruit and vegetables are sparce. Use a well-flavoured fruit (you should be able to smell its fragrance), leaving it in the fruit bowl for a few days to ripen first if necessary.

makes 1.4 kg (3 lb 2 oz)   **preparation time** 15 mins   **cooking time** 40 mins

1 large pineapple, about 1.8 kg (4 lb)

Juice of 3 lemons

750 g (1 lb 10½ oz) preserving or granulated sugar

75 g (3 oz) stem ginger, chopped

Cut away the skin from the pineapple. Remove any brown 'eyes' left on the flesh with the tip of a sharp knife. Cut the pineapple in half widthways and then vertically so you can cut away the central cores. Dice the flesh into small pieces. You should have about 1 kg (2 lb 3 oz) of pineapple flesh altogether.

Tip the pineapple into a large saucepan. Add the lemon juice and sugar and heat very gently until the sugar has dissolved and the juices are syrupy. This will take about 15–20 minutes.

Bring to the boil and cook, uncovered, for about 20 minutes until the pineapple is tender and turning translucent. Stir in the chopped ginger and cook for a further 2 minutes.

Leave to stand for 15 minutes to let the fruit settle, then ladle into sterilized jars, cover and label.

lemon curd

This is a great preserve to make when you've an excess of ripe, juicy lemons and some good-quality eggs. Besides using as a spread, lemon curd is fabulous as a filling for sponges, swirling into yogurt for an instant dessert and serving with meringues and cream.

makes 650 g (1 lb 7 oz)   **preparation time** 10 mins   **cooking time** 15 mins

Finely grated zest and juice of 3 unwaxed lemons

125 g (4½ oz) unsalted butter, cut into pieces

3 large eggs

250 g (9 oz) granulated or caster sugar

Put all the ingredients into a heatproof bowl that can rest over a saucepan of gently simmering water without the base of the bowl touching the water.

Position the bowl over the water and heat gently, whisking frequently until the butter has melted and the ingredients are smoothly combined.

Continue to stir the mixture over a gentle heat for about 15 minutes until it thickly coats the back of a wooden spoon. Press the mixture through a sieve into a clean measuring jug.

Pour into sterilized jars, cover and label.

apple, cider and rhubarb butter

Apples and rhubarb are at their best at different times of the year, but I like to make this butter in spring when rhubarb is at its most tender. Cox's are a good choice of apple, but you could use any crisp, tangy variety.

makes 700 g (1 lb 9 oz)   **preparation time** 15 mins   **cooking time** 45 mins

500 g (1 lb 2 oz) crisp dessert apples

500 g (1 lb 2 oz) young, tender rhubarb

300 ml (½ pint) strong cider

½ tsp ground cinnamon

250 g (9 oz) granulated sugar

Peel, core and roughly chop the apples. Trim and cut the rhubarb into 2 cm (¾ in) lengths. Put the fruits in a saucepan with the cider and bring to the boil. Reduce the heat and cook gently, uncovered, for about 30 minutes until the fruits are soft and pulpy. Give the fruits an occasional stir as they cook, breaking them up with a wooden spoon.

Stir in the spice and sugar and heat gently until the sugar dissolves. Continue to cook gently, stirring frequently until the mixture is thick and pulpy.

Ladle into sterilized jars, cover and label.

lime and ginger curd

This is equally as zingy as lemon curd and serves just the same purposes – sandwiching sponge cakes, topping buttery toast or folding into cream or yogurt. A delicious, zesty preserve to make in the spring, rejuvenating jaded palettes.

makes 650 g (1 lb 7 oz)   **preparation time** 15 mins   **cooking time** 20 mins

6 unwaxed limes

300 g (10½ oz) granulated or caster sugar

50 g (2 oz) piece fresh root ginger

4 large eggs

100 g (3½ oz) unsalted butter

Finely grate the lime zest and put in a food processor with the sugar. Blend until the sugar has turned a pretty pastel green. Tip half the sugar into a heatproof bowl that can rest over a saucepan of gently simmering water without the base of the bowl touching the water.

Grate the ginger onto a plate to catch the juices. (Don't worry about peeling it first as the mixture will be strained after cooking.) Add the ginger and juices to the bowl with the squeezed lime juice and eggs. Cut the butter into pieces and add to the bowl.

Position the bowl over the water and heat gently, whisking frequently until the butter has melted and the ingredients are smoothly combined.

Continue to stir the mixture over a gentle heat for about 15 minutes until it thickly coats the back of a wooden spoon. While still hot, press the mixture through a sieve into a clean measuring jug and stir in the remaining lime sugar.

Pour into sterilized jars, cover and label.

preserved lemons

Preserved lemons take on a very distinctive flavour as they mature and are used to add tang to North African and Mediterranean dishes, including salads, couscous and baked chicken and meat dishes. To use, drain from the jar and discard the juicy pulp in the centre. Wash the skin and finely shred or chop into dishes.

makes 8 preserved lemons   **preparation time** 15 mins

10 small unwaxed lemons
6 tbsp sea salt
Several bay leaves
2 tbsp multicoloured peppercorns
A little olive oil

Wash and dry the lemons. Cut 6 of the lemons lengthways into quarters or eighths, keeping them intact at one end. Sprinkle a little salt over the cut sides of the lemons.

Pack the lemons as tightly as possible into a thoroughly clean 1.5 litre (2½ pint) jar, squeezing them to fit. Tuck the bay leaves in between the lemons and sprinkle with peppercorns as you layer them up.

Sprinkle with the remaining salt and squeezed juice from the remaining lemons. Top up with cold water so the lemons are completely covered. Tap the jar several times to remove any air bubbles.

Store for 2 weeks, shaking the jar frequently, before use. Once opened, pour a little olive oil into the jar. Store in the fridge and use within 6 months.

chilli, lime and vodka jelly

Despite its non-seasonal ingredients, this potent preserve has a freshness that seems most aptly made in the spring, ready for serving with cold roast chicken, pork, leafy herb salads and creamy cheeses. Any whole pieces of fruit, vegetables, herbs or spices in a jelly naturally rise to the surface. The trick in making this one look stunning is to keep poking the pieces of lime and chilli down in the jars as the jelly sets. Eventually, the thickness of the setting jelly will stop the pieces rising.

makes approx 1.3 kg (2 lb 14 oz)   **preparation time** 20 mins, plus straining
cooking time 1¾ hours

1 kg (2 lb 3 oz) unwaxed limes, plus 1 extra to finish

2 unwaxed lemons

200 ml (7 fl oz) vodka

1 medium-strength red chilli, thinly sliced

375 g (13 oz) granulated or preserving sugar for every 500 ml (18 fl oz) strained juice

Roughly chop the 1kg (2 lb 3 oz) limes and the lemons and put in a preserving pan or large saucepan. Add 1 litre (1¾ pints) water and bring to the boil. Reduce the heat, cover and simmer very gently for about 1¼–1½ hours or until the fruit skins are very soft.

Strain the fruits and juice through a jelly bag or muslin bag suspended over a large bowl for at least 4 hours or overnight.

Thinly slice the remaining lime. Stir the vodka into the strained juice and measure the quantity. Return to the cleaned pan and add the sugar. Heat gently, stirring until the sugar has dissolved, then bring to the boil and boil for 5 minutes. Skim off any scum that rises to the surface and stir in the lime and chilli slices. Boil for a further 5–10 minutes or until setting point is reached.

Leave the jelly to stand for 20 minutes before ladling into sterilized jars. As the lime and chilli slices rise to the surface, push them down into the jelly using a thoroughly clean metal or wooden skewer until the jelly starts to thicken. Cover and label.

VARIATION A medium-strength chilli gives this jelly a mild kick. Use 1–2 hot chillies for a more fiery flavour or a milder chilli to lessen the heat. The same quantity of white rum or gin can be used instead of the vodka.

tarragon vinegar

Infusing a plain vinegar with herbs gives extra flavour as long as you use plenty to compete with the strength of the vinegar. Tarragon is a good choice as it's useful in salad dressings or in sauces such as Hollandaise, but any other herbs or mixture of herbs can be used instead.

makes 500 ml (18 fl oz)   **preparation time** 5 mins

Plenty of tarragon leaves (about 100 g/3½ oz)

500 ml (18 fl oz) white wine vinegar

Pack the tarragon leaves into a large, thoroughly clean glass bottle or several smaller ones.

Top up with the vinegar and cover with a vinegar-proof lid or stopper. Leave in a warm place for 4 weeks, shaking the bottle frequently.

Strain through a fine sieve and return to the bottle or bottles, pushing fresh sprigs of tarragon down into the vinegar, both to decorate and identify. Store in a cool place for up to 6 months.

grape, apple and rosemary jelly

This clear jelly is great with rich roasts like lamb or pork and even good in a baguette with cold sliced leftovers. Both grapes and apples are high in pectin so you won't need to boil this jelly for long before it sets. Have some jars ready and waiting.

makes approx 900 g (2 lb)   **preparation time** 15 mins, plus straining
cooking time 30 mins

700 g (1 lb 9 oz) green grapes

1 kg (2 lb 3 oz) cooking apples

4 x 18 cm (7 in) sprigs rosemary, plus extra sprigs to finish

375 g (13 oz) preserving or granulated sugar for every 500 ml (18 fl oz) strained juice

Several bay leaves

Pull the grapes from their stalks. Roughly chop the apples without peeling or coring and put both the fruits in a preserving pan or large saucepan with the rosemary. Add 1 litre (1¾ pints) water and bring to the boil. Reduce the heat, cover with a lid and simmer gently for about 15–20 minutes until the fruits are soft and pulpy.

Strain the fruits and juice through a jelly bag or muslin bag suspended over a large bowl for at least 4 hours or overnight.

Measure the strained juice. Return to the cleaned pan and add the sugar. Heat gently, stirring until the sugar has dissolved, then bring to the boil and boil for 5–10 minutes or until setting point is reached. While boiling skim off any scum that rises to the surface.

Ladle into sterilized jars, pushing a thoroughly clean, dry rosemary sprig and bay leaf down into each to decorate. Cover and label.

herb oil

Herb oils are great in mayonnaise, salad dressings and any other recipe where you might use a good olive oil. Use a single herb or a mixture of different herbs that go well together. A regular or mild olive oil is generally better than an extra virgin one, which might be too overpowering for the herbs. Decanted into glass bottles, they make very good presents.

makes 500 ml (18 fl oz)   **preparation time** 5 mins, plus standing

50 g (2 oz) basil, thyme, rosemary, oregano, fennel, tarragon, chives or parsley, plus fresh herbs to decorate the bottle

500 ml (18 fl oz) olive oil

Use a pestle and mortar (or a bowl and the end of a rolling pin) to bruise the herb, or herbs, which will help to release their flavour.

Put in a bowl or jar and add the oil. Cover and leave in a warm place such as a sunny windowsill for 2–3 weeks.

Strain through a fine sieve into a jug. Pour into one large sterilized, thoroughly dry bottle or several smaller ones. Push a few herb sprigs down into the oil, both to decorate and identify.

Cover with screw–topped lids, clip tops or stoppers and store in a cool place for up to 6 months.

sweet dill mustard

Yellow (sometimes called white) mustard seeds have a milder flavour than black ones, but can still provide quite a fiery kick! Once made the mustard will be very thin, but will thicken up overnight as the seeds absorb the vinegar. It's then best left for a week before eating so the flavour mellows, and will keep for up to three months. Dill mustard can be served with any meats and is particularly good with Gravad Lax, smoked salmon and other smoked fish.

makes 350 g (12½ oz)   **preparation time** 5 mins, plus standing

100 g (3½ oz) yellow mustard
seeds

1 tsp sea salt

1 tsp ground turmeric

50 g (2 oz) light muscovado sugar

50 g (2 oz) granulated sugar

200 ml (7 fl oz) white wine vinegar

15 g (½ oz) dill

Put the mustard seeds, salt, turmeric and sugars in a blender or food processor and blend. Alternatively, use a coffee grinder, reserved specially for spice grinding. (For a coarse grain mustard, lightly blend the seeds. For a smoother mustard blend to a powder.)

Turn into a bowl and stir in the vinegar. Cover and leave to stand overnight.

Chop the dill, discarding any tough stalks and stir into the mustard. Pack into small, thoroughly clean jars and cover with waxed circles and vinegar-proof lids.

VARIATION Use other herbs such as parsley, fennel, coriander or tarragon instead of the dill. If using tarragon, reduce the amount to 7 g (¼ oz). Alternatively, use a little grated horseradish to taste, reducing the sugar by half. Homemade mustard is lovely mixed with mayonnaise or thick yogurt for a quick and easy dip.

spicy banana and date chutney

We've become so used to a good standard of banana right through the year that we tend to take them for granted. This recipe works best for bananas that aren't too firm or too mushy but somewhere in between.

makes 1.4 kg (3 lb 2 oz)   **preparation time** 20 mins   **cooking time** 30 mins

Finely grated zest and juice of 2 unwaxed lemons

4 large bananas

1 large cooking apple, peeled, cored and finely chopped

300 g (10½ oz) pitted dates, chopped

1 onion, chopped

40 g (1½ oz) fresh root ginger, grated

½ tsp ground allspice

½ tsp ground turmeric

1 tsp salt

400 ml (14 fl oz) white wine vinegar

200 g (7 oz) granulated sugar

Put the lemon zest and juice in a preserving pan or large saucepan. Peel and slice the bananas into the pan. Add the apple and stir until the fruits are coated in the lemon juice.

Add the remaining ingredients and heat gently until the sugar dissolves. Bring to the boil, reduce the heat and simmer gently for about 30 minutes or until the mixture is thickened and pulpy.

Ladle into thoroughly clean jars, cover and label.

caramelized red onion chutney

In many recipes this is referred to as 'onion marmalade', though it's more like chutney in the way it's prepared and cooked. Serve alongside meat and game pâtés and pies, cold meats, sausages or even cheese on toast.

makes 1 kg (2 lb 3 oz)   **preparation time** 20 mins   **cooking time** 40 mins

5 tbsp olive oil

1.5 kg (3 lb 5 oz) red onions, thinly sliced

100 g (3½ oz) dark muscovado sugar

Small handful of fresh thyme, chopped

2 garlic cloves, crushed

200 ml (7 fl oz) balsamic vinegar

Juice of 1 lemon

Heat the oil in a large, deep frying pan or sauté pan. Add the onions and 2 tablespoons of the sugar and fry gently, stirring frequently until the onions are beginning to caramelize. This will take about 20 minutes. (If you only have a small frying pan, fry the onions in batches and tip them into a saucepan to finish the chutney. If you try and cook them altogether they'll steam rather than fry.)

Add the rest of the sugar, the thyme, garlic, vinegar and lemon juice and bring to the boil.

Reduce the heat and simmer gently, uncovered, for about 15–20 minutes or until the juices are thick and syrupy and the onions are moist.

Ladle into thoroughly clean jars, cover and label.

aromatic salt

Sea salt, flavoured with herbs and spices, can be used as a general seasoning for cooking and is really good for sprinkling over asparagus and other tender vegetables. It's even better with quails' eggs or sprinkled over soft-boiled or poached egg yolks – delicious!

makes 115 g (4 oz)   **preparation time** 5 mins

2 bay leaves
1 tsp freshly ground black pepper
1 tsp crushed dried chillies
1 tsp celery seeds
1 tbsp chopped rosemary
1 tbsp chopped thyme
100 g (3½ oz) sea salt

Crumble the bay leaves into a food processor or coffee grinder reserved for grinding spices. Add the pepper, chillies, celery seeds, rosemary, thyme and 1 tablespoon of the salt.

Blend until the herbs and spices are fairly finely ground. Tip into a bowl with the remaining salt and mix well.

Store in an airtight jar and use within 2 months.

VARIATION Other seeds like fennel, cumin, coriander or mustard can be added to the salt. Grind them separately and toast in a dry frying pan to bring out their flavours before adding to the salt. For a short-term aromatic salt, use soft herbs like fennel, dill, parsley, chives, tarragon and coriander and the zest of a lemon. The moisture in the herbs will gradually dissolve the salt, so it needs to be stored in the fridge and used within a few days.

hot harissa sauce

This quick and easy, fiery sauce can be used – cautiously – to add flavour to soups, stews, dressings and vegetable dishes. Mixed with canned or fresh chopped tomatoes, it makes an instant sauce for pasta.

makes 150 g (5 oz)   **preparation time** 10 mins

100 g (3½ oz) red chillies
1 small head garlic
1 tsp coriander seeds
1 tsp caraway seeds
1 tsp celery salt
1 tbsp mild paprika
4 tbsp chopped coriander
1 tbsp chopped mint
3 tbsp olive oil

Deseed and roughly chop the chillies. Skin the garlic cloves and put with the chillies in a food processor.

Toast the coriander and caraway seeds in a dry frying pan. Lightly crush using a pestle and mortar and add to the processor with the celery salt and paprika. Blend to a smooth paste, scraping down any mixture that clings to the side of the bowl.

Once the mixture has formed a fairly smooth paste, add the herbs, 2 tablespoons of the oil and 1–2 tablespoons water to make a thick sauce.

Pack the sauce into a small, sterilized jar and pour the remaining olive oil over the top to seal. Cover with an airtight lid and store in the fridge for up to 2 months.

yogurt cheese in flavoured oil

Making cheese is one of the most satisfying of all preserves and is one that can really be made at any time of year, but seems to suit spring best. It's a simple process but needs several days for straining the curds from the whey. For a short-cut version buy soft goat's cheese, cut it into small pieces, and preserve in the flavoured oil.

makes 900 g (2 lb) **preparation time** 30 mins, plus straining

750 g (1 lb 10½ oz) Greek yogurt

½ tsp salt

1½ tsp multicoloured peppercorns, crushed

Handful of lemon thyme or oregano sprigs

4 bay leaves

2 garlic cloves, thinly sliced

300 ml (½ pint) extra virgin olive oil

Soak a 30 cm (12 in) square of muslin in boiling water. Beat the yogurt in a bowl with the salt and peppercorns. Place the muslin on a plate and tip the cheese mixture onto it. Bring up the sides of the muslin and tie in a bundle with string.

Suspend the bundle by hanging it from a kitchen cupboard handle with a bowl underneath to catch the whey. Leave for about 2 days until the yogurt has stopped dripping. (If the weather is very hot, hang the bundle of yogurt from a shelf in the fridge with a bowl underneath.)

Sterilize 2 small wide-necked preserving jars. Open out the muslin and shape heaped teaspoonfuls of the cheese into balls by rolling them between the palms of your hands. Arrange in the jars, tucking in thyme or oregano sprigs, bay leaves and garlic slices as you fill the jars.

Pour over the olive oil and seal the jars. Store in the fridge and use within 1 month.

coconut, lime and chilli relish

This spicy relish is lovely with simply steamed white fish or salmon, or with chicken kebabs, barbecued pork or tofu burgers. Intensely flavoured with garlic, chilli, lemongrass and ginger, a little goes a long way. If you can't get Asian pears, use dessert pears or apples instead.

makes 800 g (1 lb 12 oz)   **preparation time** 25 mins   **cooking time** 20 mins

2 Asian pears, peeled, cored and diced

1 bunch spring onions

1 onion, chopped

1 green pepper, deseeded and finely chopped

1 red or green chilli, deseeded and finely chopped

1 stalk lemongrass, finely chopped

3 garlic cloves, finely chopped

40 g (1½ oz) fresh root ginger, finely chopped

150 ml (¼ pint) rice vinegar

Finely grated zest and juice of 2 unwaxed limes

100 g (3½ oz) granulated sugar

Grated flesh of 1 small coconut

Put the pears in a saucepan with 100 ml (3½ fl oz) water and bring to the boil. Reduce the heat, cover with a lid and cook gently for 5 minutes or until the pears are tender.

Finely chop the spring onions, keeping the white and green parts separate. Add the white spring onions to the pan with the onion, green pepper, chilli, lemongrass, garlic, ginger, vinegar, lime juice and sugar.

Bring to the boil, reduce the heat and simmer gently, uncovered, for about 15 minutes until most of the liquid has evaporated.

Stir in the grated coconut, lime zest and green parts of the spring onions. Cook for a further 2 minutes, stirring.

Pack into small, thoroughly clean jars, cover and label. Refrigerate and use within 2 months.

lemon vodka

This recipe imitates Limoncello, the zesty Italian liqueur. Serve as and when you would other liqueurs, either in small shot glasses or over crushed ice. It's also good drizzled over creamy lemon desserts and even added to a chicken or pork casserole.

makes 400 ml (14 fl oz)   **preparation time** 10 mins, plus standing

10 unwaxed lemons

250 g (9 oz) granulated sugar

300 ml (½ pint) vodka

Finely grate the zest from the lemons and put in a bowl with 75 ml (2½ fl oz) boiling water. Leave to stand for 1 hour.

Squeeze the juice from the lemons and put in a large jug with the sugar. Strain the juice from the zest into the bowl and stir well until the sugar has dissolved.

Add the vodka and pour into thoroughly clean clip or screw-topped bottles. Store in a cool place for up to 6 months.

fresh limeade

Homemade limeade bursts with flavour and really tastes of limes, ideal for an invigorating burst of sweet tanginess whenever you're in the mood. Dilute with chilled sparkling water or pour over vanilla ice cream in tall glasses, topping up with soda water.

makes 1 litre (1¾ pints)   **preparation time** 10 mins, plus standing

12 unwaxed limes

4 unwaxed lemons

400 g (14 oz) granulated sugar

2 tsp citric acid

Finely grate the zest from the limes and lemons and put in a saucepan with the sugar and 500 ml (18 fl oz) water. Heat gently until the sugar dissolves, then bring to the boil. Pour into a bowl and leave to stand for 1 hour.

Squeeze the lime and lemon juice into a large jug and strain the syrup into the juice. Stir in the citric acid.

Pour into sterilized clip or screw-topped bottles. Store in a cool place, or refrigerated, for up to 2 months. Serve diluted with still or sparkling water.

VARIATION For fresh lemonade, use 12 unwaxed lemons only.

pink ginger cordial

Plump, juicy, fresh root ginger is available all year, but spring and summer is when this invigorating cordial is just what is needed. A few blackberries give it a pastel pink tinge but they are certainly not essential to the recipe and won't affect the flavour.

makes 600 ml (1 pint)   **preparation time** 5 mins, plus standing

75 g (3 oz) fresh root ginger
1 unwaxed lemon, sliced
250 g (9 oz) granulated sugar
3 blackberries
1 tsp citric acid

Grate the ginger into a large bowl. (Don't bother to peel it first as the ingredients will be strained after soaking.) Stir in the remaining ingredients. Add 500 ml (18 fl oz) boiling water and mash the blackberries lightly against the side of the bowl to release their juices. Cover with cling film and leave to stand overnight.

Strain through a muslin-lined sieve into a large jug and pour into sterilized clip or screw-topped bottles. Store in a cool place or refrigerate, for up to 4 weeks. Serve diluted with still or sparkling water.

Summer

Early summer is the time when most gardens come to life as various flowers such as roses and lavender start to bloom. If you're after 'free food', watch for the emergence of highly fragranced, creamy white elderflower heads that make such a fabulous cordial for serving right through the summer. Gathering these herbs and flowers for preserving is best done during the morning before the heat of the sun evaporates their aromatic oils and fragrances. The first soft fruits including strawberries, raspberries, black, white and redcurrants are usually at their best in midsummer, and if you haven't time to preserve the currants straight away, they'll freeze well for when you have. Midsummer is the time to gather gooseberries and cherries, their short season making them something to really treasure in jams and conserves.

blueberry and vanilla jam

Use bought vanilla sugar for this recipe, or preserve your own by nestling a whole, split vanilla pod in a jar of sugar for several weeks. For a quicker version, thinly slice a vanilla pod and whizz it in the food processor with 100 g (3½ oz) granulated sugar until only tiny specks of the vanilla are visible.

makes 1.3 kg (2 lb 14 oz)   preparation time 10 mins   cooking time 30 mins

1 kg (2 lb 3 oz) blueberries

125 ml (4 fl oz) freshly squeezed lemon juice (juice of about 4 lemons)

800 g (1 lb 12 oz) granulated or preserving sugar

100 g (3½ oz) vanilla sugar

Tip the blueberries into a preserving pan or large saucepan. Add the lemon juice and 4 tbsp water and cook gently for about 10 minutes, stirring frequently until the blueberries are soft and mushy.

Stir in both the sugars and heat gently until the sugar dissolves.

Bring to the boil and boil for about 20 minutes until setting point is reached, skimming any scum from the surface.

Ladle into sterilized jars, cover and label.

honeyed apricots

Steeped in a golden, thyme-scented honey syrup, these preserved apricots make a lovely dessert, spooned over soft, creamy mascarpone cheese or as a topping for an almond tart. Make plenty and revel in the luxury of eating this short-seasoned fruit throughout the year.

makes 1 kg (2 lb 3 oz)   preparation time 15 mins   cooking time 25 mins

750 g (1 lb 10½ oz) apricots, halved and stoned

Handful of thyme sprigs

250 g (9 oz) clear honey

300 ml (½ pint) dry white or rosé wine

2 tbsp lemon juice

Preheat the oven to 150°C/300°F/Gas Mark 2. Pack the apricots into 2–3 sterilized, wide-necked preserving jars with a total capacity of 1.2 litres (2 pints), tucking plenty of thyme sprigs around them.

Put the honey, wine and lemon juice in a large saucepan and heat gently, stirring as you bring the syrup to a gentle simmer. Pour the honey syrup over the apricots so they are completely immersed. Tap the jars on the surface to eliminate any air bubbles. Push a thin-bladed knife or skewer down the sides of the jar to release any bubbles you can see through the glass.

Position the lids and rubber seals if using, but don't tighten the lids. Place the jar in a newspaper-lined roasting tin. Cook for 20 minutes. Remove from the oven and immediately seal the jars. Label and store for up to 6 months.

strawberry jam

As delicious as it is, strawberry jam is renowned for being difficult to set due to its low pectin level. If you've boiled the jam for a while and only get a light set when testing, leave it there. It'll have a slightly syrupy consistency but will still taste good. Boiling for too long will make the jam oversweet and caramelly, losing the fresh taste of the berries.

makes 1.8 kg (4 lb)   **preparation time** 10 mins   **cooking time** 30 mins

1.4 kg (3 lb 2 oz) strawberries, hulled

Juice of 4 lemons

1.4 kg (3 lb 2 oz) preserving or granulated sugar

Tip the strawberries into a preserving pan or large saucepan. Add the lemon juice, cover and cook gently for about 10 minutes, stirring frequently until the strawberries are soft and mushy.

Stir in the sugar and heat gently until the sugar dissolves.

Bring to the boil and boil for about 15–20 minutes until setting point is reached, skimming any scum from the surface.

Ladle into sterilized jars, cover and label.

raspberry jam

This is such an easy jam to make as there's no preparation (other than checking over the raspberries first) and it sets fairly easily. If you want a quick, decisive set, a good variation is to use half raspberries and half redcurrants, which are high in pectin.

makes 1.9 kg (4 lb 3 oz)   **preparation time** 5 mins   **cooking time** 20 mins

1 kg (2 lb 3 oz) raspberries

1 kg (2 lb 3 oz) preserving or granulated sugar

Juice of 2 lemons

Tip the raspberries into a preserving pan or large saucepan and cook gently in their own juice, stirring frequently, until they're soft and turning mushy.

Stir in the sugar and lemon juice and heat gently until the sugar dissolves.

Bring to the boil and boil for about 15 minutes until setting point is reached, skimming any scum from the surface.

Ladle into sterilized jars, cover and label.

apricot jam

The kernels inside apricot stones are edible and are often added to apricot preserves for their slightly almondy flavour. The stones need cracking with a hammer or nutcracker, which can be fiddly but is worth the effort. If you're having trouble extracting the kernels, leave them out.

makes 1.5 kg (3 lb 5 oz)   **preparation time** 20 mins   **cooking time** 35 mins

1 kg (2 lb 3 oz) apricots

Juice of 1 lemon

1 kg (2 lb 3 oz) preserving or granulated sugar

Halve and stone the apricots. Crack open the stones, take out the kernels and peel off the skins. If the skins don't come away easily, blanch the kernels in boiling water for 1 minute to loosen them.

Put the apricots, kernels, lemon juice and 300 ml (½ pint) water in a preserving pan or large saucepan. Bring to the boil, reduce the heat and cover with a lid. Cook very gently for 15–20 minutes until the apricots are soft.

Stir in the sugar and heat gently until the sugar has dissolved. Bring to the boil and boil for about 15 minutes until setting point is reached.

Leave to stand for 10 minutes to let the fruit settle. Ladle into sterilized jars, cover and label.

peach and redcurrant jam

To make a low pectin fruit such as peaches into a successful jam, they need to be combined with a high pectin one such as redcurrants. This combination is practical, delicious and a very pretty addition to the storecupboard.

makes 2.4 kg (5¼ lb)   **preparation time** 20 mins   **cooking time** 15 mins

1 kg (2 lb 3 oz) ripe, juicy peaches

1 kg (2 lb 3 oz) redcurrants

Juice of 2 lemons

1.4 kg (3 lb 2 oz) preserving or granulated sugar

Put the peaches in a large heatproof bowl. Cover with boiling water and leave for 1 minute. Drain off the water and peel away the skins from the peaches. Halve, discard the stones and roughly chop the flesh.

Strip the redcurrants from their stalks by running them between the tines of a fork.

Put the fruits in a preserving pan or large saucepan with the lemon juice and 100 ml (3½ fl oz) water. Bring to the boil, reduce the heat and simmer very gently, covered, for about 5 minutes until the fruits are soft.

Stir in the sugar and heat gently until the sugar has dissolved. Bring to the boil and boil for about 10 minutes until setting point is reached.

Leave to stand for 10 minutes to let the fruit settle. Ladle into sterilized jars, cover and label.

gooseberry and elderflower jam

Gooseberries have one of the shortest seasons of all the summer fruits, ripening in midsummer, then disappearing altogether. Nature obviously intended that the flavours of gooseberries and elderflower complement each other, as they're both ripe and ready at the same time.

makes 1.6 kg (3½ lb)   **preparation time** 15 mins   **cooking time** 25 mins

1 kg (2 lb 3 oz) gooseberries, topped and tailed

Finely grated zest and juice of 1 lemon

900 g (2 lb) preserving or granulated sugar

6–8 elderflower heads, chopped, with tough stalks removed

Tip the gooseberries into a preserving pan or large saucepan with the lemon zest and juice and 150 ml (¼ pint) water. Cook gently, uncovered, for about 15 minutes until the gooseberries are tender and pulpy.

Stir in the sugar and heat gently until the sugar dissolves.

Stir in the elderflower heads and bring to the boil. Boil for about 10 minutes until setting point is reached, skimming any scum from the surface.

Ladle into sterilized jars, cover and label.

blackcurrant jam

Tangy, aromatic blackcurrants simply burst with flavour and make a jam that's one of the quickest 'setters' of all. Make sure you have your jars ready and waiting! If you don't have time to make the jam once you've bought or picked the fruit, they freeze well for a jam-making session later on.

makes 1.6 kg (3½ lb)   **preparation time** 15 mins, plus standing
cooking time 5 mins

1 kg (2 lb 3 oz) blackcurrants

1.2 kg (2 lb 10½ oz) preserving or granulated sugar

Strip the blackcurrants from their stalks by running them between the tines of a fork.

Put in a large bowl and prick them all over with a fork to release some of the juices. Stir in the sugar and leave for 2–3 hours until the juices have started to run and the sugar is turning syrupy.

Tip into a preserving pan or large saucepan and heat gently until all the sugar has dissolved. Bring to the boil and boil for about 5 minutes until setting point is reached, skimming any scum from the surface.

Ladle into sterilized jars, cover and label.

redcurrant jelly

Unless you're lucky enough to produce home-grown redcurrants, try buying them from summer farmers' markets rather than the tiny tubs of supermarket redcurrants that are so expensive. Commercial redcurrant jelly can be oversweet and thickly set, whereas a fresh, fruity homemade version is as good for topping buttered bread as it is for accompanying roast lamb.

makes approx 650 g (1 lb 7 oz)   **preparation time** 15 mins, plus straining
cooking time 35 mins

900 g (2 lb) redcurrants

375 g (13 oz) preserving or granulated sugar for every 500 ml (18 fl oz) juice

Put the redcurrants in a preserving pan or large saucepan with 300 ml (½ pint) water. There's no need to remove the stalks from the redcurrants as the fruit will be strained after cooking.

Bring to the boil and simmer gently, covered with a lid, for 20–25 minutes until the redcurrants are very soft and pulpy.

Strain the fruit and juice through a jelly bag or muslin bag suspended over a large bowl for at least 4 hours or overnight.

Measure the strained juice. Return to the cleaned pan and add the sugar. Heat gently, stirring until the sugar has dissolved, then bring to the boil and boil for about 10 minutes or until setting point is reached. While boiling skim off any scum that rises to the surface.

Ladle into sterilized jars, cover and label.

soft fruit and lavender jelly

This soft set, summery jelly has a subtle hint of lavender. It's great with shortcake or scones and cream, and can be used instead of redcurrant jelly for glazing summer tarts.

makes approx 1.5 kg (3 lb 5 oz)   **preparation time** 15 mins, plus straining
cooking time 40 mins

1.4 kg (3 lb 2 oz) mixture of strawberries, raspberries and redcurrants

Juice of 4 lemons

15 lavender flowers, plus extra to decorate

375 g (13 oz) preserving or granulated sugar for every 500 ml (18 fl oz) juice

Put all the fruits in a preserving pan or large saucepan. (There's no need to hull or string the fruits as the pulp will be strained after cooking.) Add the lemon juice, their pulp and pips left in the squeezer, the lavender flowers and 750 ml (1¼ pints) water. Bring to the boil, cover with a lid and reduce the heat. Cook gently for 20 minutes until the fruits are soft and pulpy.

Strain the fruit and juice through a jelly bag or muslin bag suspended over a large bowl for at least 4 hours or overnight.

Measure the strained juice. Return to the cleaned pan and add the sugar. Heat gently, stirring until the sugar has dissolved, then bring to the boil and boil for about 20 minutes or until setting point is reached. While boiling skim off any scum that rises to the surface.

Ladle into sterilized jars. As the jelly starts to thicken, several sprigs of lavender flowers can be pushed down into it to decorate. Cover and label.

cherry and orange conserve

Although cherries have a very short season, this preserve enables you to enjoy them right through the year. The orange and liqueur flavouring adds a lovely tang to the sweetness of the fruit, perfect for spooning over chocolate or vanilla ice cream, or topping warm scones.

makes 1.2 kg (2 lb 10½ oz)   **preparation time** 20 mins   **cooking time** 40 mins

1 kg (2 lb 3 oz) black or red cherries, pitted

700 g (1 lb 9 oz) preserving or granulated sugar

Juice of 2 oranges

Juice of 1 lemon

6 tbsp Cointreau or other orange-flavoured liqueur

Tip the cherries into a large saucepan and add the sugar, orange and lemon juice. Heat gently, stirring frequently until the sugar has dissolved.

Stir in the liqueur and bring to the boil, making sure all the sugar has dissolved before turning up the heat.

Reduce the heat to a gentle simmer and cook, uncovered, for about 40 minutes until the juices are reduced and the liquid is thick and syrupy.

Leave in the pan for 20 minutes before ladling into sterilized jars, cover and label.

rose petal and apple conserve

Use scented pink or red 'garden' roses, rather than bought ones for this recipe, picking them during the morning of a dry day before the aromatic oils have escaped. Adding a small beetroot to the conserve during cooking will compensate for the slight dulling of colour to the rose petals.

makes 850 g (1 lb 14 oz)   **preparation time** 20 mins   **cooking time** 15 mins

100 g (3½oz) heavily scented roses

750 g (1 lb 10½oz) cooking apples, peeled, cored and roughly chopped

400 g (14 oz) preserving or granulated sugar

1 tbsp lemon juice

1 small raw beetroot, quartered

2 tbsp rosewater

Pull all the rose petals from the stalks and tear into small pieces. Put in a saucepan with the apples. Add 150 ml (¼ pint) water and cook gently, covered with a lid, until the apples start to soften, about 5 minutes.

Stir in the sugar, lemon juice and beetroot and heat gently until the sugar dissolves. Bring to the boil and lift out the pieces of beetroot. Boil for about 10 minutes or until thick and pulpy

Remove from the heat and stir in the rosewater. Ladle into sterilized jars, cover and label.

peach and apple jelly

Soft, sweet, juicy peaches are one of summer's special treats. For those of us who can't boast a thriving peach tree or good local supply, we have to buy instead. Often hard and somewhat tasteless, peaches, like many other fruits, will improve in texture and flavour if left at room temperature for a few days. This jelly is lovely with summery roast pork or chicken and can liven up leftovers the next day. If nectarines look riper and juicier than the peaches, use them instead.

makes approx 1.2kg (2lb 10½oz)   **preparation time** 15 mins, plus straining
cooking time 55 mins

6 large, ripe peaches

1 kg (2 lb 3 oz) crisp dessert apples

2 unwaxed lemons

Small handful of lemon thyme or sage, plus extra to finish

375 g (13 oz) preserving or granulated sugar for every 500 ml (18 fl oz) strained juice

Halve and roughly chop the peaches, apples and lemon and put in a preserving pan or large saucepan with the herbs and 450 ml (¾ pint) water. (There's no need to remove the stones or cores as the fruits will be strained after cooking.) Bring to the boil, cover with a lid and reduce the heat. Cook very gently for about 45 minutes until the fruits are soft and pulpy.

Strain the fruit and juice through a jelly bag or muslin bag suspended over a large bowl for at least 4 hours or overnight.

Measure the strained juice. Return to the cleaned pan and add the sugar. Heat gently, stirring until the sugar has dissolved, then bring to the boil and boil for about 10 minutes or until setting point is reached. While boiling skim off any scum that rises to the surface.

Ladle into sterilized jars. As the jelly starts to thicken, several sprigs of thyme or sage can be pushed down into the jelly to decorate. Cover and label.

saffron and apricot jelly

Saffron always adds such an exotic touch to the simplest recipes. This beautiful, amber-coloured preserve can be spooned over soft cheeses like ricotta or goat's cheese or served with thick yogurt, whipped cream or even meringues. The quantity made will vary, depending on the firmness of the apricots used.

makes approx 700 g (1 lb 9 oz)   **preparation time** 15 mins, plus straining
cooking time 35 mins

900 g (2 lb) apricots

Juice of 2 lemons

375 g (13 oz) preserving or granulated sugar for every 500 ml (18 fl oz) strained juice

1 tsp saffron strands

Halve the apricots, without removing the stones. Put in a preserving pan or large saucepan with the lemon juice and 400 ml (14 fl oz) water. Bring to the boil, reduce the heat, cover and simmer gently for about 20 minutes or until the apricots are soft and pulpy.

Strain the fruit and juice through a jelly bag or muslin bag suspended over a large bowl for at least 2 hours or overnight.

Measure the strained juice. Return to the cleaned pan and add the sugar. Heat gently, stirring until the sugar has dissolved.

Bring to the boil and boil for about 15 minutes until setting point is reached. While boiling skim off any scum that rises to the surface. Turn off the heat and crumble in the saffron strands.

Leave to stand for 15 minutes, stirring occasionally. This will help prevent the saffron from rising to the top of the jelly. Stir again and ladle into sterilized jars, cover and label.

soft fruit and drambuie butter

Butters are easier to make than jams as you don't need to worry about boiling and setting. Simply cook the purée until thick and pulpy, bearing in mind that it'll thicken slightly as it cools. This butter's lovely with scones and cream or any other recipe where you might use a red fruit jam. If you don't want to use Drambuie, use another liqueur, or freshly squeezed orange juice instead.

makes 600 g (1 lb 5 oz)   **preparation time** 15 mins   **cooking time** 35 mins

800 g (1 lb 12 oz) mixture of soft fruits, such as strawberries, raspberries, redcurrants, blackcurrants and blackberries

300 g (10½ oz) granulated sugar

5 tbsp Drambuie

Put all the fruits in a large saucepan. Don't bother to hull the fruits or remove stalks as they'll be strained after cooking. Add 150 ml (¼ pint) water and bring to the boil. Reduce the heat, cover with a lid and simmer gently for 20 minutes or until the fruits are soft and pulpy.

Press the fruit and juice through a sieve and return to the cleaned pan.

Stir in the sugar and liqueur and heat gently until the sugar has dissolved. Continue to cook, stirring frequently, for about 15 minutes until thick and pulpy.

Ladle into sterilized jars, cover and label.

raspberry and mint curd

Even slightly imperfect raspberries can be used for this recipe, such as unique-shaped home-grown ones or those that have got squashed when picking. It also works well with blackberries, loganberries and mulberries later in the year.

makes 750 g (1 lb 10½ oz)   **preparation time** 10 mins   **cooking time** 25 mins

400 g (14 oz) raspberries

10 large sprigs mint

250 g (9 oz) granulated or caster sugar

125 g (4½ oz) unsalted butter, cut into pieces

5 medium eggs

Blend the raspberries in a food processor or blender to a purée. Press through a sieve into a large heatproof bowl to extract the seeds. Use a pestle and mortar (or a small bowl and the end of a rolling pin) to bruise the mint sprigs and add to the bowl with the sugar, butter and eggs.

Position the bowl over a saucepan of gently simmering water, making sure that the base of the bowl does not touch the water. Heat gently, whisking frequently until the butter has melted and the ingredients are smoothly combined.

Continue to stir the mixture over a gentle heat for about 15 minutes until it thickly coats the back of a wooden spoon. Press the mixture through a sieve into a clean measuring jug.

Pour into sterilized jars, cover and label.

summer fruits in mulled rosé

These fruits are preserved by 'bottling' in the oven, which extends their storage time for up to about six months. For short-term storage, there's no need to cook fruits in the jars. Instead, seal the jars at the end of step 4 and refrigerate for up to two weeks.

makes 1.5 kg (3 lb 5 oz)   **preparation time** 20 mins   **cooking time** 30 mins

1 kg (2 lb 3 oz) mixture of strawberries, raspberries and redcurrants

400 ml (14 fl oz) rosé wine

2 tbsp brandy or orange-flavoured liqueur

125 g (4½ oz) caster or granulated sugar

1 cinnamon stick, halved

12 whole cloves

25 g (1 oz) piece fresh root ginger, very thinly sliced

Preheat the oven to 150°C/300°F/Gas Mark 2. Hull the strawberries, halving any large ones. Remove the redcurrants from their stalks.

Pack the fruits into 2 or 3 sterilized, wide-necked preserving jars with a 1.5 litre (2½ pint) total capacity.

Put the wine in a saucepan with the liqueur, sugar and spices and heat gently until the sugar has dissolved. Heat until almost boiling. Pour over the fruits, filling the jars right up to the necks.

Tap the jars on the surface to remove any air bubbles, or push a fine-bladed knife or skewer down the sides of the jars to release any air bubbles that you can see through the glass.

Position the lids and rubber seals if using but don't tighten the lids. Space the jars, well apart, in a newspaper-lined roasting tin. Cook for 20 minutes. Remove from the oven and immediately seal the jars. Label and store for up to 6 months.

olives marinated in provençal oil

Use this recipe if you've bought 'plain' olives and want to give them more flavour. They'll keep in the fridge for a couple of months and the oil, once the olives are eaten, will give a lovely flavour to salad dressings.

makes 250 g (9 oz)   **preparation time** 10 mins

2 tsp fennel seeds, lightly crushed

½ tsp celery seeds

2 tsp coriander seeds

250 g (9 oz) black or green olives in brine

Several strips of pared orange zest

3 bay leaves, lightly crushed

1 small garlic clove, crushed

4 tbsp chopped parsley

¼ tsp freshly ground black pepper

Approx 200 ml (7 fl oz) olive oil

Put all the seeds in a dry frying pan and heat gently until lightly toasted. Leave to cool.

Put the olives in a bowl and scatter with the seeds, orange zest, bay leaves, garlic, parsley and pepper. Stir together until mixed.

Pack the ingredients into sterilized jars, tucking the bay leaves and orange zest among the olives.

Pour over enough olive oil to completely submerge the olives. Cover and refrigerate.

green olive and peppercorn sauce

This is such an easy, well-flavoured sauce to make, and one that's delicious to dip into whenever you fancy it. Serve, crostini-style, spread on to toasted rustic bread, or toss with fresh pasta for a simple supper. It's also lovely as an accompaniment to roasted vegetables and egg dishes or any dishes where you might use tapenade.

makes 500 g (1 lb 2 oz)   **preparation time** 10 mins

100 g (3½ oz) blanched almonds

325 g (11½ oz) pitted green olives, drained and rinsed if bottled in brine

2 small garlic cloves, roughly chopped

2 tbsp lemon juice

125 ml (4 fl oz) olive oil, plus a little extra

4 tsp green peppercorns in brine, lightly crushed

4 tbsp chopped parsley

Blend the almonds in a food processor until ground. Tip out into a bowl.

Put the olives in the processor with the garlic, lemon juice, olive oil and peppercorns and blend until smooth, scraping down any pieces that cling to the sides of the bowl.

Return the almonds to the food processor and process until very smooth. Add the parsley and blend lightly to mix.

Pack the paste into small sterilized and cooled jars and level the surface. Drizzle with a little olive oil to seal.

Cover with screw-topped lids and store in a cool place for up to 6 months.

courgettes in walnut oil

This preserve is great if you're trying to keep up with glut supplies of home-grown courgettes that start appearing in the summer, growing at a rate that is impossible to consume as a fresh vegetable. They're perfect for snacking on and make a quick and easy starter, piled on a bed of chicory with a scattering of sliced goat's cheese.

makes about 750 g (1 lb 10½ oz)   **preparation time** 25 mins, plus brining
cooking time 20 mins

1 kg (2 lb 3 oz) courgettes
50 g (2 oz) salt
Approx 350 ml (12 fl oz) walnut oil
100 g (3½ oz) walnut pieces
Finely grated zest of 2 lemons
3 garlic cloves, crushed
15 g (½ oz) tarragon leaves, chopped

Cut the courgettes diagonally into 5 mm (¼ in) slices and layer up in a colander, sprinkling each layer with salt. Leave to stand for 2 hours. Rinse the courgettes in plenty of water to remove all traces of salt. Drain on kitchen paper.

Season 3 tablespoons of the oil with plenty of pepper and brush over one side of the courgette slices. Heat a griddle and cook the courgettes, oiled side face down until seared on the underside. Brush the tops with more oil, turn the slices and cook until the undersides are golden. You'll probably need to do several batches depending on the size of the griddle. If you don't have a ridged griddle use a regular frying pan.

Sterilize wide-necked preserving jars with a 750 ml (1¼ pint) total capacity.

Layer up the courgettes and walnut pieces in the jars, seasoning the layers and sprinkling in the lemon zest, garlic and tarragon leaves. Pour over the remaining walnut oil, shaking the jars to remove any air pockets. Make sure the courgettes are completely covered with oil. Cover and refrigerate for up to 2 months.

cucumber, dill and mustard pickle

The delicate greens and pinks of the cucumber and red onions give this preserve plenty of visual appeal, though the colours do gradually tone down during storage. Served straight from the jar with a chunk of cheese or cold meats and some grainy bread, it makes such a simple, tasty lunch.

makes about 1 kg (2 lb 3 oz)   **preparation time** 20 mins, plus brining

2 large cucumbers (about 900 g/2 lb)

2 red onions, thinly sliced

6 tbsp sea salt

2 tbsp mustard seeds

2 tsp celery seeds

25 g (1 oz) dill, finely chopped

600 ml (1 pint) white wine vinegar

175 g (6 oz) granulated sugar

Thinly slice the cucumbers and layer up in a colander with the onions and sea salt. Leave to stand for 2 hours. Rinse well and leave to drain.

Heat the mustard seeds and celery seeds in a saucepan until the mustard seeds start to pop. Tip the cucumbers and onions into a bowl and mix in the seeds and dill. Pack the mixture into thoroughly clean, wide-necked preserving jars with a total capacity of about 1.5 litres (2½ pints).

Put the vinegar and sugar in a saucepan and heat gently until the sugar had dissolved. Pour into the jars, cover and label. Store in a cool place for up to 9 months.

elderflower cordial

Commercial elderflower cordial is available all year but nothing beats the flavour, and satisfaction, of making your own. Made in early summer when elderflowers are abundant, it provides a fresh, summery infusion to take you right through the summer and beyond.

makes about 1.5 litres (2½ pints) **preparation time** 5 mins, plus standing

20 large elderflower heads
3 unwaxed lemons, sliced
25 g (1 oz) citric acid
1 kg (2 lb 3 oz) granulated sugar

Mix the elderflower heads, lemon slices and citric acid together in a large bowl. Dissolve the sugar in 1 litre (1¾ pints) boiling water and add to the bowl. Cover with cling film and leave to stand for 24 hours.

Strain through a muslin-lined sieve into a large jug and pour into sterilized clip or screw-topped bottles. Store in a cool place, or refrigerated, for up to 6 weeks. Serve diluted with still or sparkling water.

soft fruit cordial

A delicious and healthier alternative to shop-bought fruit squash and a great use for soft summer fruits in cheap supply, or any that are too squashy for eating. Don't use too many dark red fruits as they'll overpower the colour and flavour of the subtler ones.

makes 750 ml (1¼ pints) **preparation time** 10 mins, plus standing

750 g (1 lb 10½ oz) mixture of soft fruits, such as strawberries, raspberries, red or blackcurrants, blackberries or mulberries
225 g (8 oz) granulated sugar
1 tsp tartaric or citric acid

Lightly blend the fruits, in batches, in a food processor until mushy. (Don't bother to hull the fruits or remove redcurrant stalks first.) Turn into a large bowl and stir in 200 ml (7 fl oz) boiling water. Cover with cling film and leave to stand for 1 hour.

Strain the pulp through a sieve into a bowl, pressing the pulp with the back of a spoon to extract as much juice as possible.

Put the sugar in a saucepan with 100 ml (3½ fl oz) water. Pour over the fruit juice and stir in the tartaric or citric acid.

Pour into sterilized clip or screw-topped bottles. Store in a cool place, or refrigerated, for up to 6 weeks. Serve diluted with still or sparkling water.

VARIATION For Apple and Blackberry Cordial, use a mixture of blackberries and chopped dessert apples instead of the soft fruits. Make as above.

cherry and almond ratafia

Fresh cherries are at their best during the summer when they're in abundant supply at farmers' markets and farm shops, even from roadside stalls. This 'ratafia' liqueur is made by steeping the cherries with almonds in sweetened brandy so that, over time, the flavours meld together perfectly. Don't waste the strained cherries and almonds – drenched in brandy they're great in trifle, fruit cakes or almond tarts, while the liqueur makes a gorgeous aperitif, served over crushed ice.

makes 350 ml (12 fl oz)   **preparation time** 10 mins, plus standing

50 g (2 oz) blanched almonds, roughly chopped

300 g (10½ oz) cherries, halved and stoned

75 g (3 oz) caster sugar

300 ml (½ pint) brandy

Lightly toast the almonds and put in a thoroughly clean screw-topped jar with the cherries and sugar. Shake the jar to mix the ingredients together.

Add the brandy and leave to stand for 2 days, shaking the jar occasionally to dissolve the sugar. Store in a cool place for 3 months.

Strain through a muslin-lined sieve into a jug, reserving the fruit and nuts. Pour the liqueur into a thoroughly clean, clip or screw-topped bottle. The fruit and nuts can be served with cream and a drizzle of the liqueur, or added to trifle, fruit cakes or almond-flavoured tarts.

Store the liqueur for up to 6 months and serve in small glasses or over crushed ice.

raspberry vinegar

Raspberry vinegar gives a fresh summery flavour to salad dressings or, when used in small quantities, to zip up the pan juices after frying red meats or game. Use up raspberries that are mushy or slightly past their best for eating fresh.

makes 500 ml (18 fl oz)   **preparation time** 5 mins

400 g (14 oz) raspberries

500 ml (18 fl oz) red wine vinegar

2 tbsp granulated or caster sugar

Use a wooden spoon to mash up the raspberries in a bowl.

Add the vinegar. Cover and leave to stand for 5 days, stirring occasionally.

Strain through a fine sieve and stir in the sugar. Pour into a thoroughly clean bottle or several smaller bottles. Cover with a vinegar-proof lid or stopper and store in a cool place for up to 12 months.

VARIATION Almost any soft fruits can be used in fruit vinegars. Try strawberries, redcurrants, blackcurrants, blackberries or mulberries. Pink peppercorns and warm spices such as cinnamon sticks and whole cloves can also be added to the vinegar.

Autumn

Autumn provides a preserver's paradise – glut supplies of fruit and vegetables to harvest and pot into jams, jellies, chutneys, relishes and pickles. Now's the time to reap the rewards of nurturing a vegetable plot, or to go foraging in the woods and hedgerows for sloes, brambles, damsons and other seasonal treats that are ripe and ready for picking. Tomatoes are at their best, great in ketchup and chutney, they also make a delicious marmalade. Pumpkins, squash, courgettes and marrows are now in glorious abundance and there's plenty around for eating fresh or preserving. Best of all are the orchard fruits, now at the height of their season, including sweet juicy plums, apples, pears and mulberries. Quince are harder to find unless you've grown your own, but are well worth seeking out for their sweet, honeyed flavour.

plum jam

Most plum varieties cook and set quickly so this is a pretty easy jam to master. It's also good for yellow plums, damsons or greengages, although greengages are slightly lower in pectin and might need longer cooking.

makes 1.5 kg (3 lb 5 oz)   **preparation time** 10 mins   **cooking time** 25 mins

1 kg (2 lb 3 oz) plums, halved and stoned

1 kg (2 lb 3 oz) preserving or granulated sugar

Put the plums in a preserving pan or large saucepan with 150 ml (¼ pint) water. Cook gently, uncovered, for about 15 minutes until the plums are tender and pulpy.

Stir in the sugar and heat gently until the sugar dissolves.

Bring to the boil and boil for about 10 minutes until setting point is reached, skimming any scum from the surface.

Ladle into sterilized jars, cover and label.

blackberry and apple jam

This is one of the most perfect fruit combinations and works as well in a jam as any other recipe. It makes a lovely topping for warm scones, drop scones or as a filling for little jam tarts, or for simply spreading on buttered bread.

makes 2.1 kg (4 lb 10 oz)   **preparation time** 15 mins   **cooking time** 25 mins

700 g (1 lb 9 oz) blackberries

750 g (1 lb 10½ oz) cooking apples, peeled, cored and chopped

Juice of 2 lemons

1.3 kg (2 lb 14 oz) preserving or granulated sugar

Put the blackberries and apples in a preserving pan or large saucepan with the lemon juice and 100 ml (3½ fl oz) water. Cover and cook gently for about 15 minutes until the fruits are soft and pulpy, stirring frequently.

Stir in the sugar and heat gently until the sugar has dissolved. Bring to the boil and boil for 5–10 minutes until setting point is reached.

Leave to stand for 10 minutes to let the fruit settle. Ladle into sterilized jars, cover and label.

bramble jelly

Finding food for free is so satisfying, particularly when you can make it into something that's going to last for months. Wild brambles have quite a long season, first appearing in late summer with later crops that can last up to late autumn. Pick them when you get the chance, even if it means collecting a tubful in the freezer until you've got enough. Blackberries make an equally flavour-packed substitute if you don't have a laden supply of hedgerows!

makes 1 kg (2 lb 3 oz)   **preparation time** 20 mins   **cooking time** 30 mins

1 kg (2 lb 3 oz) brambles

1 kg (2 lb 3 oz) preserving or granulated sugar

Juice of 2 lemons

Rinse the brambles and put in a preserving pan or large saucepan with 400 ml (14 fl oz) water. There's no need to remove any stalks as the fruit will be strained after cooking.

Bring to the boil, reduce the heat and cover with a lid. Cook gently for about 20 minutes until the fruit is soft and pulpy.

Stir in the sugar and lemon juice and heat gently until the sugar has dissolved. Bring to the boil and boil rapidly for 5–10 minutes until setting point is reached.

Put a metal sieve over a large, heatproof glass jug or bowl and ladle the jelly into it. Press the jelly through the sieve with the back of a large, metal spoon, until all the juice has been extracted. Discard the pulp.

Ladle into sterilized jars, cover and label.

crab apple jelly

Early autumn is generally the time for making crab apple jelly. Small, hard and sour, crab apples don't ripen like dessert apples, but their high pectin content contributes to make an easy set jelly with a stunning colour. Serve with gammon and bacon, or with roast pork as a seasonal change from apple sauce.

makes approx 1.4 kg (3 lb 2 oz)   **preparation time** 15 mins, plus straining
cooking time 1¾ hours

2 kg (4 lb 6 oz) crab apples

1 tsp whole cloves

375 g (13 oz) preserving or granulated sugar for every 500 ml (18 fl oz) strained juice

Roughly chop the crab apples and put in a preserving pan or large saucepan with the cloves and 1.75 litres (3 pints) cold water. Bring to the boil, cover with a lid and reduce the heat. Cook very gently for about 1¼–1½ hours until the apples are soft and pulpy.

Strain the fruit and juice through a jelly bag or muslin bag suspended over a large bowl for at least 4 hours or overnight.

Measure the strained juice. Return to the cleaned pan and add the sugar. Heat gently, stirring until the sugar has dissolved, then bring to the boil and boil for about 10 minutes or until setting point is reached. While boiling skim off any scum that rises to the surface.

Ladle into sterilized jars, cover and label.

mulled plum jelly

This is a great jelly to make in the autumn, ready for wintry cooking. It's perfect with roasted poultry and game, or with festive cured meats, or even with a cheeseboard. Gently softened in a small pan, it makes a sticky glaze for plum tart.

makes approx 1.8 kg (4 lb)   **preparation time** 15 mins, plus straining
cooking time 45 mins

1.8 kg (4 lb) plums

Juice of 3 lemons

1 tbsp whole cloves

3 cinnamon sticks

75 g (3 oz) fresh root ginger, thinly sliced

300 ml (½ pint) red wine

375 g (13 oz) preserving or granulated sugar for every 500 ml (18 fl oz) strained juice

Halve the plums but don't worry about removing the stones. Put in a preserving pan or large saucepan with the lemon juice, the pulp and pips left in the squeezer, cloves, cinnamon, ginger and 1 litre (1¾ pints) water. Bring to the boil, then reduce the heat. Cook gently, uncovered, for 25 minutes until the plums are soft and pulpy.

Strain the fruit and juice through a jelly bag or muslin bag suspended over a large bowl for at least 4 hours or overnight.

Add the wine to the strained juice and measure the quantity. Return to the cleaned pan and add the sugar. Heat gently, stirring until the sugar has dissolved, then bring to the boil and boil for about 20 minutes or until setting point is reached. While boiling skim off any scum that rises to the surface.

Ladle into sterilized jars, cover and label.

quince jelly

This pretty-coloured jelly is perfect with red meats and game and can be stirred into the roasting pan juices to sweeten and flavour the gravy. Quinces have a high pectin content so the jelly should set fairly quickly.

makes approx 650 g (1 lb 7oz)   **preparation time** 15 mins, plus straining **cooking time** 1¼ hours

1 kg (2 lb 3 oz) quinces

Juice of 2 lemons

375 g (13 oz) preserving or granulated sugar for every 500 ml (18 fl oz) strained juice

Roughly chop the quinces. There's no need to peel or core them as the fruit will be strained after cooking. Put in a preserving pan or large saucepan with the lemon juice and 1 litre (1¾ pints) water. Bring to the boil, cover with a lid and reduce the heat. Cook gently for about 1 hour until the fruit is soft and pulpy.

Strain the fruit and juice through a jelly bag or muslin bag suspended over a large bowl for at least 4 hours or overnight.

Measure the strained juice. Return to the cleaned pan and add the sugar. Heat gently, stirring until dissolved, then bring to the boil and boil for about 10 minutes or until setting point is reached. While boiling skim off any scum that rises to the surface.

Ladle into sterilized jars, cover and label.

minted apple jelly

Cider vinegar adds a tangy, savoury flavour to this jelly that's perfect for accompanying rich meats like lamb, duck and goose. Quantities can easily be doubled up if you've a good source of home-grown apples.

makes approx 1.4 kg (3 lb 2 oz)   **preparation time** 25 mins, plus straining **cooking time** 45 mins

1 kg (2 lb 3 oz) cooking apples

Handful of mint sprigs

600 ml (1 pint) cider vinegar

375 g (13 oz) preserving or granulated sugar for every 500 ml (18 fl oz) strained juice

Roughly chop the apples, without peeling or coring, and put in a preserving pan or large saucepan with a couple of mint sprigs and 600 ml (1 pint) water. Bring to the boil, reduce the heat, cover and cook gently for 20–30 minutes until soft and pulpy. Add the vinegar and cook for a further 5 minutes.

Strain the fruit and juice through a jelly bag or muslin bag suspended over a large bowl for at least 4 hours or overnight.

Measure the strained juice. Return to the cleaned pan and add the sugar. Heat gently, stirring until the sugar has dissolved, then bring to the boil and boil for about 10 minutes or until setting point is reached. While boiling skim off any scum that rises to the surface.

Finely chop the remaining mint and stir into the jelly. Leave to stand for 15 minutes, then stir lightly. This will help prevent the chopped mint from rising to the top of the jelly.

Ladle into sterilized jars, cover and label.

pear, lemon and cardamom marmalade

The warm spiciness of cardamom is often paired with citrus fruits in sweet and savoury dishes, adding a slightly exotic flavour. The lightly crushed seeds look pretty, suspended in the set jelly, but if you don't fancy picking them out when serving, tie them in the muslin bag instead, so their flavour infuses the fruits.

makes 2.3 kg (5 lb)   **preparation time** 40 mins   **cooking time** 1¾ hours

800 g (1 lb 12 oz) unwaxed lemons

1 kg (2 lb 3 oz) firm pears (such as Conference), peeled, cored and roughly chopped

2 tbsp cardamom pods

1.3 kg (2 lb 14 oz) preserving or granulated sugar

Halve and squeeze the lemons. Cut the squeezed lemons in half. Using a sharp knife, flatten the peel down on the surface and cut a thick horizontal slice to remove the pith from the peel. Tie the pith in a large square of muslin with the pips. Shred the peel as thinly as possible.

Put the muslin bag in a preserving pan or large saucepan with the squeezed juice, shredded peel and 1.5 litres (2½ pints) water. Bring to the boil, reduce the heat and cover with a lid. Cook very gently for 1 hour. Add the chopped pears and cook, covered, for a further 20 minutes until the pieces of lemon are very tender and the pears are soft.

Crush the cardamom pods using a pestle and mortar to open the pods and expose the seeds.

Lift out the muslin bag from the pan, pressing it against the side to squeeze out as much juice as possible. Discard the bag. Add the crushed cardamom pods to the pan with the sugar and heat gently until the sugar dissolves. Bring to the boil and boil until setting point is reached, about 20–25 minutes. Leave to stand for 20 minutes to allow the pieces of fruit to settle.

Ladle into sterilized jars, cover and label.

tomato marmalade

Unconventional, but sweet and distinctively tomato flavoured, this preserve is brilliant against the saltiness of bacon or breakfast sausages. It makes a fairly small quantity but can easily be doubled up if you've a large supply of ripe tomatoes.

makes 1.2 kg (2 lb 10½ oz)   **preparation time** 25 mins
cooking time 1½ hours

1.2 kg (2 lb 10½ oz) ripe tomatoes
2 oranges
2 unwaxed lemons
800 g (1 lb 12 oz) granulated or preserving sugar

Put the tomatoes in a large heatproof bowl, cover with boiling water and leave for 30 seconds to 2 minutes until the skins split. Drain, skin and roughly chop the tomatoes and put in a preserving pan or large saucepan. Cook, uncovered, for about 12–15 minutes until the tomatoes are broken up and the juices are thick and pulpy.

Coarsely grate the zest from the oranges and lemons and put the gratings in a medium saucepan. Squeeze the juice, reserving the pips, and tip the juice and pulp into the saucepan. Roughly chop the skins and tie in a square of muslin with the pips. Add to the pan with 400 ml (14 fl oz) water. Bring to the boil, cover and reduce the heat. Cook very gently for 1 hour.

Remove the muslin bag, pressing it against the side of the pan to remove as much juice as possible. Discard the bag.

Tip the fruit syrup into the tomato pan and stir in the sugar. Heat gently until the sugar dissolves. Bring to the boil and boil until setting point is reached, about 15 minutes.

Ladle into sterilized jars, cover and label.

simple apple chutney

Apple chutney is one of the easiest and simplest of all, but you can still give it a little twist by introducing some less obvious spices. Chinese five spice, with its slightly exotic flavour, is a good choice, but mixed spice or a sprinkling of cloves or allspice can be used instead for an even simpler version.

makes 1.5 kg (3 lb 5 oz)   **preparation time** 15 mins   **cooking time** 30 mins

1.5 kg (3 lb 5 oz) cooking apples, peeled, cored and roughly chopped

150 g (5 oz) raisins

500 g (1 lb 2 oz) onions, chopped

4 tsp five spice powder

1 tbsp ground ginger

300 g (10½ oz) granulated sugar

300 ml (½ pint) cider vinegar

Put all the ingredients in a preserving pan or large saucepan.

Heat gently, stirring until the sugar dissolves, then bring to the boil. Reduce the heat and simmer gently, uncovered, for about 30 minutes or until the mixture is thick and pulpy. Give the chutney an occasional stir to stop it sticking to the base.

Ladle into thoroughly clean jars, cover and label.

damson cheese

This tangy preserve contrasts perfectly in flavour and texture with smooth, creamy goat's cheeses, Brie and Camembert. It also makes a fabulous treat served with freshly baked bread or muffins and a dollop of clotted cream.

makes about 1.4 kg (3 lb 2 oz)   **preparation time** 15 mins
cooking time 1 hour

1.4 kg (3 lb 2 oz) damsons

350 g (12½ oz) granulated or caster sugar for every 600 ml (1 pint) purée

Put the damsons in a large saucepan with 150 ml (¼ pint) water and bring to the boil. Reduce the heat, cover with a lid and simmer gently for about 25 minutes until the fruit is soft and pulpy.

Press the fruit and juice through a sieve, using the back of a metal spoon to extract as much pulp as possible. Measure the purée. Return to the cleaned pan and add the sugar.

Cook over a gentle heat until the sugar has dissolved, then cook for a further 30 minutes or until the mixture is very thick. A wooden spoon, drawn across the base of the pan should leave a clear line through the mixture.

Ladle into sterilized jars, cover and label.

chilli tomato chutney

This recipe requires lots of well-flavoured, ripe tomatoes. Use glut supplies, either home-grown or from a market when they are more likely to be a bargain buy. Even slightly over-ripe, squidgy ones that you might no longer want in a salad are fine. Two chillies make it quite fiery, one is much milder, but you can, of course, leave the chilli out altogether.

makes 1.2 kg (2 lb 10½ oz)   **preparation time** 20 mins   **cooking time** 40 mins

2 kg (4 lb 6 oz) tomatoes
2 tbsp black onion seeds
2 tbsp mustard seeds
2 hot Thai red chillies, deseeded and finely chopped
2 large onions, chopped
4 garlic cloves, crushed
2 tsp celery salt
175 g (6 oz) granulated sugar
150 ml (¼ pint) cider vinegar

Put the tomatoes in a large heatproof bowl, cover with boiling water and leave to stand for 30 seconds to 2 minutes or until the skins start to split. (The steeping time will depend on the tomatoes, very ripe ones won't need as long.) Drain, peel away the skins and roughly chop the tomatoes. Tip into a preserving pan or large saucepan.

Put the onion seeds and mustard seeds in a frying pan and heat for 1–2 minutes until the mustard seeds start to pop. Add to the pan.

Add all the remaining ingredients and heat gently stirring with a wooden spoon until the juices start to run from the tomatoes. Continue to cook, uncovered, for a further 30–40 minutes until most of the liquid has evaporated and the mixture is thick and pulpy. Give the mixture an occasional stir to stop the tomatoes sticking.

Ladle into thoroughly clean jars, cover and label.

pumpkin and ginger chutney

Make this in autumn during the short season that pumpkin is widely available to buy, unless, of course, you have a home-grown supply. If you can't get hold of good-quality pumpkin, squash can be used instead.

makes 1.9 kg (4 lb 3 oz)   **preparation time** 20 mins   **cooking time** 50 mins

1 kg (2 lb 3 oz) skinned and deseeded piece pumpkin

500 g (1 lb 2 oz) onions, chopped

100 g (3½ oz) raisins

75 g (3 oz) fresh root ginger, grated

1 tsp salt

2 cinnamon sticks

½ tsp ground cloves

2 tbsp coriander seeds, lightly crushed

500 ml (18 fl oz) white wine vinegar

375 g (13 oz) light muscovado sugar

Good pinch saffron strands

Cut the pumpkin into small chunks and put in a preserving pan or large saucepan with the remaining ingredients.

Heat gently until the sugar dissolves. Bring the mixture to the boil, reduce the heat and cook, covered with a lid, until the pumpkin starts to soften. Uncover and simmer gently for about 40 minutes or until the mixture is thick and pulpy. Stir the mixture frequently to prevent it sticking to the base of the pan.

Ladle into thoroughly clean jars, cover and label.

moroccan spiced plum chutney

'Ras el Hanout' is a Moroccan spice blend that includes pepper, coriander, paprika, cardamom, allspice, nutmeg and cloves. If you can't get hold of any, you could always mix a few of the above spices from your storecupboard.

makes 1.4 kg (3 lb 2 oz)   **preparation time** 20 mins   **cooking time** 30 mins

900 g (2 lb) red or yellow plums

375 g (13 oz) onions, chopped

50 g (2 oz) piece fresh root ginger, finely chopped

100 g (3½ oz) pitted dates, chopped

1 cinnamon stick

1 tsp ground turmeric

1 tbsp cumin seeds, lightly crushed

300 ml (½ pint) white wine vinegar

100 g (3½ oz) granulated sugar

2 tsp Ras el Hanout Moroccan spice blend

75 g (3 oz) pine nuts, toasted

Halve and roughly chop the plums, discarding the stones. Put the plums in a preserving pan or large saucepan with the remaining ingredients except the spice blend and pine nuts.

Cook gently, stirring frequently until the sugar has dissolved. Bring to the boil, then reduce the heat and cook gently, uncovered, for 10 minutes until the plums are turning pulpy. Add the spice blend and pine nuts and cook for a further 20 minutes or until the chutney is thick and pulpy. Fish out the cinnamon stick and discard.

Ladle the chutney into thoroughly clean jars, cover and label.

aubergine, walnut and smoked garlic chutney

Smoked garlic is widely available and has a more subtle flavour than regular garlic, hence the large quantity used in this recipe.

makes 1 kg (2 lb 3 oz)   **preparation time** 25 mins   **cooking time** 45 mins

300 g (10½ oz) aubergines, cut into 1 cm (½ in) dice

3 onions, finely chopped

300 g (10½ oz) cooking apples, peeled, cored and chopped

100 g (3½ oz) sultanas

1 bulb smoked garlic, cloves skinned and sliced

1 tsp ground cinnamon

1 tsp hot chilli powder

1 tbsp cumin seeds, lightly crushed

½ tsp ground turmeric

1 tsp salt

250 g (9 oz) light muscovado sugar

350 ml (12 fl oz) white wine or cider vinegar

100 g (3½ oz) toasted walnuts, chopped

Put all the ingredients except the walnuts in a preserving pan or large saucepan and heat gently, stirring until the sugar dissolves.

Bring to the boil, reduce the heat and simmer very gently, uncovered, until the mixture is thick and pulpy. This will take about 30–40 minutes. Stir the chutney frequently to prevent the mixture sticking to the base.

Add the walnuts and cook gently for a further 5 minutes.

Ladle into thoroughly clean jars, cover and label.

red pepper and coriander relish

Colourful and mildly spiced, this relish is great with barbecued meats, sausages and burgers. Quantities can easily be doubled as it's the kind of sauce you'll get through quickly!

makes 800 g (1 lb 12 oz)   **preparation time** 15 mins   **cooking time** 30 mins

700 g (1 lb 9 oz) red peppers, deseeded and finely chopped

300 g (10½ oz) tomatoes, skinned and chopped

2 red onions, finely chopped

200 ml (7 fl oz) red wine vinegar

75 g (3 oz) light muscovado sugar

1 tsp celery salt

1 tsp hot smoked paprika

15 g (½ oz) chopped coriander

Place all the ingredients except the coriander in a large saucepan and bring to the boil. Reduce the heat and cook very gently, uncovered, for about 25 minutes until the liquid has evaporated but the mixture is still moist.

Stir in the coriander until well distributed and cook for 2 minutes.

Ladle into thoroughly clean jars, cover and label.

jalapeño chilli and corn relish

For a quick snack, spoon this relish onto tortilla chips, sprinkle with grated Cheddar or Gruyère and lightly grill to soften the cheese. It's also perfect with steaks, burgers and sausages. For a child-friendly version try halving the Jalapeño chillies.

makes 1 kg (2 lb 3 oz)   **preparation time** 20 mins   **cooking time** 25 mins

3 corn cobs, husks and silks removed

1 small head fennel, finely chopped

2 celery sticks, finely chopped

50 g (2 oz) bottled Jalapeño chillies, drained and chopped

400 g (14 oz) can chopped tomatoes

250 ml (9 fl oz) white wine vinegar

2 garlic cloves, chopped

100 g (3½ oz) granulated sugar

¼ tsp salt

Cook the corn cobs in boiling water for 5 minutes. Drain and leave until cool enough to handle. Remove the corn from the core by holding the cob upright on a plate and making vertical cuts with a knife. Put the corn in a food processor and blend very briefly so the kernels are broken up but not pulpy.

Tip the corn into a saucepan and add all the remaining ingredients. Bring to the boil, reduce the heat and simmer gently, uncovered, for about 20 minutes until most of the liquid has evaporated and the vegetables are still a little crunchy.

Ladle into thoroughly clean jars, cover and label.

pickled beetroot and red cabbage

makes 1.5 kg (3 lb 5 oz)   **preparation time** 20 mins, plus brining
cooking time 1 hour

1 small red cabbage, about 700 g
(1 lb 9 oz)

75 g (3 oz) salt

600 g (1 lb 5 oz) beetroot

850 ml (1½ pints) cider vinegar

2 tbsp pickling spice

3 tbsp light muscovado sugar

1 tbsp juniper berries, crushed

Thinly slice the cabbage, discarding the core, and put in a bowl. Add the salt and mix with your hands until the cabbage is coated in salt. Cover and leave to stand for 24 hours.

Cook the whole beetroot in simmering water until softened but still quite firm in the centre, about 40 minutes. Drain and when cool enough to handle, peel away the skins. Cut into thin slices.

Put the cider vinegar, pickling spice and sugar in a saucepan and bring to a gentle simmer. Cover and cook gently for 15 minutes.

Arrange alternate layers of the cabbage and beetroot in thoroughly clean, wide-necked preserving jars with a 1.5 litre (2½ pint) total capacity. Scatter in the juniper berries as you fill the jars.

Strain the spiced vinegar and pour over the vegetables, making sure they're completely immersed in the vinegar. Cover and label. Store in a cool place for up to 9 months.

pickled garden vegetables

makes 1.8 kg (4 lb)   **preparation time** 30 mins, plus brining
cooking time 25 mins

1.4 kg (3 lb 2 oz) prepared mixed
garden vegetables such as marrow,
cucumber, carrots, French beans,
baby onions and cauliflower

125 g (4½ oz) salt

1 tbsp cumin seeds,
lightly crushed

1 tbsp coriander seeds,
lightly crushed

1 tsp crushed dried chillies

1 tbsp black onion seeds

1 tbsp mustard powder

450 ml (¾ pint) white wine vinegar

200 g (7 oz) granulated sugar

25 g (1 oz) fresh root ginger, grated

2 garlic cloves, crushed

25 g (1 oz) plain flour

To prepare the vegetables, peel and remove the seeds from the marrow and cucumber. Trim and slice the beans into 2 cm (¾ in) lengths. Peel the onions and leave whole. Cut the cauliflower into small florets. Weigh the vegetables, making sure you have about 1.4 kg (3 lb 2 oz).

Put the vegetables in a large bowl with the salt. Cover with cold water and rest a plate over the top to keep the vegetables immersed in the brine. Leave to stand for 24 hours.

Rinse the vegetables in several changes of cold water to remove all traces of salt. Leave to drain.

Put the crushed spices in a preserving pan or large saucepan with the onion seeds and mustard and heat gently for a couple of minutes until lightly toasted. Add 400 ml (14 fl oz) of the vinegar, the sugar, ginger and garlic and heat until the sugar has dissolved.

Tip in the drained vegetables and bring to the boil. Reduce the heat and simmer gently, covered with a lid, for 15–20 minutes until the vegetables have softened slightly. Blend the remaining vinegar with the flour and add to the pan. Cook, stirring for a further 5 minutes, until the juices have thickened.

Ladle into thoroughly clean jars, cover and label. Store in a cool place for up to 9 months.

whole pickled chillies

If you buy a large quantity of chillies from a market and only use one or two, it's worth pickling the rest as they'll keep for up to six months. Remove from the jar as you need them, rinse and use as you would fresh, though of course they will have a slightly softer texture.

makes 250 g (9 oz)   **preparation time** 10 mins   **cooking time** 2 mins

250 g (9 oz) red, green or mixed chillies

300 ml (½ pint) white wine vinegar

6 garlic cloves, thinly sliced

2 tbsp coriander seeds

3 bay leaves or kaffir lime leaves

1 lemongrass stalk, halved lengthways

4 tbsp granulated sugar

Prick the chillies all over several times using a cocktail stick or fine metal skewer. Bring a saucepan of water to the boil. Add the chillies and return to the boil. Boil for 1 minute, then drain the chillies and refresh in cold water. Drain well.

Put the vinegar in a saucepan with the garlic, coriander seeds, lime leaves, lemongrass and sugar. Heat gently until the sugar dissolves and bring almost to the boil.

Pack the drained chillies into a thoroughly clean 600 ml (1 pint) wide-necked preserving jar. Pour over the infused vinegar, tucking the spices and leaves around the edges. If necessary cut the lemongrass pieces in half so they fit in the jar.

Push a knife down inside the jar to release any air bubbles. Cover and store in a cool place.

vanilla pickled plums

Pickling fruits in a sweetened vinegar gives them a sweet and sour flavour that's perfect with baked or boiled hams, roast pork and crackling, tossed in salads, with game meats or served with smoked fish dishes.

makes 1 kg (2 lb 3 oz)　**preparation time** 20 mins　**cooking time** 15 mins

2 vanilla pods

325 ml (11 fl oz) red wine vinegar

300 g (10½ oz) granulated sugar

1 kg (2 lb 3 oz) plums, halved and stoned

Split the vanilla pods open with the tip of a knife and scrape out the seeds. Put the pods, seeds, vinegar and sugar in a large saucepan and heat gently until the sugar dissolves.

Add the plums and cook gently, covered, for about 10 minutes until the plums are very tender.

Drain the plums and pack into thoroughly clean, wide-necked preserving jars with a 1.5 litres (2½ pint) total capacity. Halve the vanilla pods and tuck around the fruits.

Pour the syrup over the fruits, making sure they're completely submerged. Cover and store in a cool place for up to 3 months.

baby onions in balsamic vinegar

Onions are the vegetable we take most for granted – they're always around, never expensive and are rarely the focus of any dish. Home growers, however, know how deliciously sweet and succulent they can be. In this recipe baby onions are preserved in a sweet and sour balsamic vinegar, infused with herbs and lightly sweetened. The result is more mellow and less eye-wateringly sharp than regular pickled onions!

makes 1 kg (2 lb 3 oz)　**preparation time** 15 mins, plus brining
cooking time 3 mins

1 kg (2 lb 3 oz) baby onions or shallots

100 g (3½ oz) salt

250 ml (9 fl oz) balsamic vinegar

250 ml (9 fl oz) white wine vinegar

4 bay leaves, plus extra to finish

Several sprigs of thyme, plus extra to finish

150 g (5 oz) granulated sugar

Put the unpeeled onions in a bowl and sprinkle with the salt. Add just enough cold water to cover and place a plate on top to make sure the onions are immersed in the water. Leave to stand for 24 hours.

Drain the onions from the brine and peel away the skins. (Only cut off the roots from the onions so they don't fall apart when cooked.)

Put the vinegars in a saucepan with the herbs and sugar and heat gently until the sugar has dissolved. Add the onions and bring to the boil. Reduce the heat and cook gently for 2 minutes.

Drain the onions with a slotted spoon and pack them into thoroughly clean, small, wide-necked preserving jars. Tuck fresh bay leaves and thyme sprigs in among the onions. Strain the vinegar and pour over the onions so they're completely immersed. Cover and label. Store in a cool place for up to 9 months.

saffron pickled pears

Poached pears have a tendency to rise up in the syrup once bottled. It helps if you bottle them in two or three smaller jars, rather than one large one, as long as the total capacity is about 750 ml (1¹/₄ pint). These pears are delicious served with hot or cold duck or sliced into salads such as goat's cheese, watercress and walnut.

makes about 1 kg (2 lb 3 oz)   **preparation time** 25 mins
cooking time 20 mins

10 cardamom pods
2 unwaxed lemons
300 ml (½ pint) cider vinegar
300 g (10½ oz) granulated sugar
½ tsp saffron strands
1 kg (2 lb 3 oz) firm, sweet pears, peeled, cored and halved

Using a pestle and mortar, crush the cardamom pods to open them. Pare the zest from the lemons using a citrus zester or a canelle knife. Squeeze the juice. Put the juice in a saucepan with the cardamom pods, vinegar, sugar and saffron and heat gently until the sugar dissolves.

Add the pear halves and cook gently, uncovered, until the pear halves are tender. This will take about 15 minutes.

Drain the pears and pack into thoroughly clean, wide-necked preserving jars, arranging some so the cut sides are up against the glass.

Add the lemon zest to the syrup and cook until reduced by about a quarter. Pour over the fruits so they're completely immersed. Cover and label. Store in a cool place for up to 3 months.

roasted peppers in cider vinegar

Use red peppers only in this recipe, or replace a few with green, orange or yellow ones, depending on how much colour you want to add. Scatter them over salads, pizzas or into toasted cheese and basil sandwiches. They're also good for pepping up tomato sauces and vegetable dishes.

makes 1 kg (2 lb 3 oz)   **preparation time** 20 mins   **cooking time** 50 mins

1.3 kg (2 lb 14 oz) peppers

Handful of oregano

Approx 300 ml (½ pint) cider vinegar

50 g (2 oz) granulated sugar

Preheat the oven to 200°C/400°F/Gas Mark 6. Deseed the peppers and cut into quarters. Scatter in a large roasting tin and roast for 45 minutes, turning the pieces once or twice until the peppers have softened and are beginning to brown.

Pull the oregano leaves from the stalks and scatter over the peppers. Return to the oven for a further 5 minutes. Remove from the oven and pack the peppers into sterilized, wide-necked preserving jars with a 750 ml (1¼ pint) total capacity.

Put the vinegar and sugar in a saucepan and heat until the sugar dissolves. Pour over the peppers, making sure they're completely covered with vinegar. Seal and store in a cool place. Use within 3 months.

oven-dried tomatoes in fennel oil

This is a perfect preserve for a decent quantity of sweet, well flavoured tomatoes. Shred them into salads and tomato sauces or pack into sandwiches, not forgetting to use up the flavour-packed oil in salad dressings.

makes 2 x 250 ml (9 fl oz) jars   **preparation time** 15 mins
cooking time 4 hours

1 kg (2 lb 3 oz) very ripe tomatoes, halved

1 tsp caster sugar

½ tsp dried oregano

2 garlic cloves, crushed

½ tsp celery salt

1 tbsp fennel seeds, lightly crushed

2 tbsp capers, rinsed and drained

½ tsp freshly ground black pepper

300 ml (½ pint) mild olive oil

Preheat the oven to 120°C/250°F/Gas Mark ½. Arrange the tomatoes, cut sides face up, in a baking parchment-lined roasting tin. Mix the sugar with the oregano, garlic and celery salt and sprinkle over the tomatoes with your fingers. Cook for 4 hours or until the tomatoes are shrivelled and feel quite dry.

Pack the tomatoes into sterilized, wide-necked preserving jars with a 500 ml (18 fl oz) total capacity.

Heat the fennel seeds in a dry frying pan for 2 minutes. Sprinkle over the tomatoes along with the capers and pepper. Pour over the oil to cover the tomatoes completely. Cover with lids and refrigerate for up to 2 months.

smokey barbecue sauce

This well-flavoured sauce really can make a difference to the humblest of sausage and burger barbecues. It's smooth and spicy, but if you prefer a chunkier sauce, don't blend it before bottling and use wide-necked preserving jars.

makes 1 litre (1¾ pints)   **preparation time** 25 mins
cooking time 40 mins, plus sterilizing

500 g (1 lb 2 oz) ripe tomatoes

2 tbsp olive oil

2 onions, roughly chopped

2 carrots, roughly chopped

2 garlic cloves, chopped

1 tsp celery salt

500 g (1 lb 2 oz) cooking apples, peeled, cored and roughly chopped

2 tbsp grainy mustard

2 tbsp Worcester sauce

1 tbsp hot smoked paprika

75 ml (3 fl oz) red wine vinegar

50 g (2 oz) dark muscovado sugar

Put the tomatoes in a large heatproof bowl, cover with boiling water and leave to stand for 30 seconds to 2 minutes or until the skins split. (The time will depend on the tomatoes, very ripe ones won't need as long.) Drain, peel away the skins and roughly chop the tomatoes.

Heat the oil in a large saucepan and fry the onions and carrots for 10 minutes until softened.

Stir in the remaining ingredients, including the tomatoes, mixing the ingredients together well. Cover and cook gently for about 30 minutes until the sauce is soft and pulpy.

Blend the sauce in a food processor and tip into a jug. Pour into sterilized preserving bottles with screw or clip tops, leaving a 2 cm (¾ in) space at the top of the bottles. (You'll need a total capacity of 1 litre/1¾ pint.)

Sterilize the filled bottles (see page 16). Label and store in a cool place for up to 3 months.

tomato ketchup

This recipe shows just how simple the best ketchup is to make and it is well worth making when you've a good supply of delicious, thoroughly ripe tomatoes. You can of course spice it up with chilli or smoked paprika, or add a sprinkling of chopped herbs.

makes 1.2 litres (2 pints)   preparation time 20 mins

cooking time 50 mins, plus sterilizing

1.3 kg (2 lb 14 oz) ripe tomatoes, roughly chopped

2 onions, roughly chopped

125 g (4½ oz) light muscovado sugar

1 garlic clove, crushed

¼ tsp cayenne pepper

1 tsp salt

150 ml (¼ pint) red wine vinegar

Put all the ingredients into a preserving pan or large saucepan. Bring to the boil and reduce the heat to a gentle simmer.

Cook, uncovered, for about 45 minutes until the mixture is soft and pulpy. Stir the ingredients frequently to ensure they don't stick to the base of the pan.

Press the mixture through a sieve, pressing the pulp through with the back of a metal spoon. Return to the cleaned pan.

Bring to the boil and remove from the heat. Pour into sterilized clip or screw-topped bottles, leaving a 2 cm (¾ in) space at the top of the bottles. Sterilize the filled bottles (see page 16) and use within 6 months.

chinese plum sauce

Plum sauce is traditionally served with Chinese savoury pastries and duck dishes, but is also perfect as a dipping sauce or accompaniment to pan-fried meats and game, or as a treat with early autumn barbecues.

makes 600 ml (1 pint)   preparation time 20 mins

cooking time 30 mins, plus sterilizing

500 g (1 lb 2 oz) plums, halved and stoned

1 large cooking apple, peeled, cored and roughly chopped

1 red chilli, deseeded and roughly sliced

100 ml (3½ fl oz) rice wine vinegar

1 garlic clove, roughly chopped

1 tsp five spice powder

150 g (5 oz) light muscovado sugar

Put the plums, cooking apple, chilli, vinegar, garlic and five spice powder in a saucepan with 100 ml (3½ fl oz) water. Bring to the boil, cover with a lid and reduce the heat. Simmer gently for about 20 minutes until the fruit is soft and pulpy.

Press through a sieve into a clean saucepan, pushing as much pulp through as possible.

Stir in the sugar and heat gently until the sugar has dissolved. Bring to the boil and boil for 5 minutes. Pour into sterilized clip or screw-topped bottles with a 600 ml (1 pint) total capacity, leaving a 2 cm (¾ in) space at the top of the bottles. Cover and sterilize the filled bottles (see page 16). Unopened bottles will keep in a cool place for 6 months.

bramble cassis

The merest dash of blackcurrant-flavoured Cassis liqueur is classically added to white wine to make 'Kir'. If the wine is Champagne it's known as 'Kir Royale'. Cassis is also great for adding a gentle kick to soft fruit salads, mousses and soufflés. This homemade variation is a rewarding use for wild brambles. If not available, use blackberries or blackcurrants.

makes 350 ml (12 fl oz) **preparation time** 10 mins, plus standing

225 g (8 oz) brambles
150 ml (¼ pint) brandy or vodka
75 g (3 oz) caster sugar

Crush the brambles either by mashing them in a bowl or by whizzing briefly in a food processor. Put with the brandy or vodka in a large, thoroughly clean screw-topped jar and store in a cool place for 1 month.

Strain through a muslin-lined sieve into a jug, squeezing out as much juice as possible. Stir in the sugar. Return to the cleaned jar and leave for a couple of days, shaking the jar occasionally until the sugar has dissolved.

Pour into a thoroughly clean clip or screw-topped bottle and store for up to 6 months.

VARIATION For a non-alcoholic version, use red grape juice instead of the liqueur and only steep the fruit overnight. Once made, store in the fridge for up to 2 weeks. Use in recipes as above, or add a dash to chilled sparkling water, grape or apple juice.

mulberry wine

The mulberry tree is quite unique in that the fruits appear in the spring as the new foliage unfurls, but then take months to plump up, sweeten and ripen, ready for harvesting in the autumn. This sweet, fruity liqueur can be served as an early evening tipple, or kept for next spring as a cooling iced aperitif.

makes 450 ml (³/₄ pint) **preparation time** 5 mins, plus standing

500 g (1 lb 2 oz) mulberries
100 g (3½ oz) caster sugar
200 ml (7 fl oz) dessert wine
1 vanilla pod, split lengthways

Put the mulberries in a thoroughly clean lidded container with the sugar, wine and vanilla pod.

Shake the container to mix the ingredients together, then leave to stand for several days, shaking the jar frequently until the sugar has dissolved. Store in a cool place for 1 month.

Strain through a muslin-lined sieve into a jug, then pour the liqueur into a thoroughly clean clip or screw-topped bottle. Store in a cool place.

Winter

It's surprising how much good produce is available for preserving in the winter. It might not be home-grown, but there's always something to preserve for boosting storecupboard supplies. Fruits such as cranberries, pomegranates and figs make fabulous pickles, jams, jellies and chutneys. Nuts are also in good supply and have far more potential than we give them credit. Bathed in caramel, syrup or sweet conserves, they're prefect for drizzling over cakes, pastries, cream or ice cream. Winter is also traditional marmalade-making time. Bitter Seville oranges are around for such a short spell in late winter that it's worth snatching them up when you see them. If there's no time for spontaneous preserving, freeze them whole for a later date.

chestnut conserve

This delicious conserve can be stored for several months in a cool place and served as a topping for thick yogurt, with meringues and cream or spooned over melting vanilla ice cream.

makes about 1 kg (2 lb 3 oz)   **preparation time** 10 mins
cooking time 45 mins

1 kg (2 lb 3 oz) sweet chestnuts or 600 g (1 lb 5 oz) ready-cooked frozen or vacuum-packed chestnuts

Finely grated zest and juice of 1 lemon

1 vanilla pod, split lengthways

400 g (14 oz) granulated sugar

4 tbsp whisky or rum

Make a slit into each chestnut and put in a pan of boiling water. Cook for about 5 minutes to soften, then drain and leave to cool. Peel off the shells and inner, thin skins. (Skip this step if you are using ready-cooked frozen or vacuum-packed chestnuts.)

Put the chestnuts in a large saucepan with just enough water to cover them. Bring to the boil, reduce the heat and cover with a lid. Simmer gently for about 20 minutes until very tender.

Drain about half the chestnuts using a slotted spoon and blend to a paste in a food processor. Return to the pan with the lemon zest and juice, vanilla pod and sugar. Heat gently until the sugar dissolves. Raise the heat a little and cook until the mixture is thickened and turning pulpy.

Scoop out the vanilla pod and scrape out the seeds. Return these to the pan with the whisky or rum and cook for a further 5–10 minutes until thick and pulpy.

Ladle into sterilized jars, cover and label.

cranberry jelly with winter spices

Supplies of fresh cranberries disappear from the shops in mid-winter, so buy them when they are available and freeze them for later use. Cranberries are a high-pectin fruit so you can always count on a good set.

makes approx 900 g (2 lb)   **preparation time** 10 mins, plus straining
cooking time 25 mins

1 kg (2 lb 3 oz) fresh or frozen cranberries

1 cinnamon stick

15 g (½ oz) star anise

1 tbsp whole cloves

1 dried chilli

375 g (13 oz) granulated sugar for every 500 ml (18 fl oz) strained juice

Put the cranberries in a preserving pan or large saucepan with the cinnamon, star anise, whole cloves, chilli and 750 ml (1¼ pints) water. Bring to the boil, reduce the heat, cover with a lid and simmer gently for 15 minutes until the cranberries have completely collapsed. (They'll make a popping sound as the skins split.)

Strain the fruits and juice through a jelly bag or muslin bag suspended over a large bowl for at least 4 hours or overnight.

Measure the strained juice. Return to the cleaned pan and add the sugar. Heat gently, stirring until the sugar has dissolved, then bring to the boil and boil for 5–10 minutes or until setting point is reached. While boiling skim off any scum that rises to the surface.

Ladle into sterilized jars. If liked, push a whole star anise, cinnamon stick and dried chilli down into each jar when the jelly starts to thicken. Cover and label.

tangerine jelly with star anise

Like most citrus jellies, this one's great with any rich meats, cutting through the fat with its fresh, tangy kick. It's also vaguely marmalade-like, so is naturally good on toast! Any other type of orange can be used, but tangerines, at their best, simply burst with flavour.

makes approx 1 kg (2 lb 3 oz)   **preparation time** 15 mins, plus straining
cooking time 1½ hours

900 g (2 lb) tangerines

15 g (½ oz) star anise

375 g (13 oz) preserving or granulated sugar for every 500 ml (18 fl oz) strained juice

Thoroughly wash the tangerines. Chop into small pieces and put in a preserving pan or large saucepan with the star anise, making sure all the juices go into the pan as well. There's no need to remove any pulp or pips as the fruit will be strained after cooking.

Add 1.5 litres (2½ pints) water and bring to the boil. Cover with a lid and cook gently for about 1¼ hours or until the tangerine peel is very tender.

Strain the fruits and juice through a jelly bag or muslin bag suspended over a large bowl for at least 4 hours or overnight.

Measure the strained juice. Return to the cleaned pan and add the sugar. Heat gently, stirring until the sugar has dissolved, then bring to the boil and boil for about 10 minutes or until setting point is reached. While boiling skim off any scum that rises to the surface.

Ladle into sterilized jars, cover and label.

spiced pomegranate jelly

This recipe makes a fairly small quantity, but it can be potted in small jars so you can store it away and treat yourself now and again. It is richly flavoured and aromatically spiced, perfect with smoked meats, particularly duck, and game pâtés.

makes 750 g (1 lb 10½ oz)   **preparation time** 25 mins, plus straining
cooking time 45 mins

6 large juicy pomegranates

400 g (14 oz) cooking apples

10 g (⅓ oz) star anise,
plus extra to finish

2 cinnamon sticks

450 ml (¾ pint) pomegranate juice,
plus a little extra if necessary

450 g (1 lb) granulated or
preserving sugar

Cut the pomegranates in half and break each half open into a large saucepan, pressing the clusters of seeds into the pan. Lift out any large pieces of white membrane but don't worry about the smaller pieces as the fruit will be strained after cooking.

Roughly chop the apples without peeling or coring and add to the pan with the star anise, cinnamon sticks and pomegranate juice.

Bring to the boil and reduce the heat to a gentle simmer. Cover and cook very gently for 15–20 minutes or until the apples have become mushy.

Strain the fruits and juice through a jelly bag or muslin bag suspended over a large bowl for at least 4 hours or overnight.

Measure the strained juice and top up to 600 ml (1 pint) if necessary with a little extra pomegranate juice. Return to the cleaned pan and add the sugar. Heat gently, stirring until the sugar has dissolved, then bring to the boil and boil for 20–30 minutes or until setting point is reached. While boiling skim off any scum that rises to the surface.

Ladle into sterilized jars. As the jelly starts to set add a whole star anise to each jar. Cover and label.

ruby orange marmalade

Sliced ruby oranges, or blood oranges as they're sometimes called, reveal flesh that can be familiarly orange with reddish specks or the deepest, darkest burgundy. The colour pales when made into marmalade, resulting in more of a deep amber colour.

makes 1.4 kg (3 lb 2 oz)   **preparation time** 30 mins
cooking time 1 hour 40 mins

1 kg (2 lb 3 oz) ruby oranges

2 unwaxed lemons

1.2 kg (2 lb 10½ oz) granulated or preserving sugar

Using a sharp knife, cut away the thin layer of peel, but not the white pith, from the oranges and lemons. Shred the peel finely, or alternatively chop it in the food processor and reserve.

Roughly chop the whole fruits, including the skins, and tip into a preserving pan or large saucepan. Add 1.5 litres (2½ pints) water and bring to the boil. Reduce the heat, cover with a lid and simmer gently for 50–60 minutes until the pith is very tender. Tip the contents of the pan into a large sieve, set over a bowl to catch the juice. Press the pulp in the sieve with the back of a spoon to extract as much juice as possible. Pour all the juice into the cleaned preserving pan or saucepan and discard the pulp.

Add the shredded or chopped peel to the pan and bring to the boil. Reduce the heat, cover and simmer gently for 25 minutes until the peel is very tender.

Stir in the sugar and heat gently until dissolved. Bring to the boil and boil until setting point is reached, about 15 minutes.

Leave to stand for 20 minutes to allow the peel to settle, then ladle into sterilized jars. Cover and label.

seville orange marmalade

Seville oranges are only available for a few weeks, from mid- to late winter. Their bitter flavour gives marmalade a distinctive tang that can't be achieved using other types of oranges.

makes 1.2 kg (2 lb 10½ oz)   **preparation time** 25 mins   **cooking time** 1¾ hours

1 kg (2 lb 3 oz) Seville oranges

Juice of 2 lemons

1.8 kg (4 lb) preserving or granulated sugar

Using a sharp knife, cut away the thin layer of peel, but not the white pith, from the oranges. Shred the peel thinly or thickly, depending on personal preference.

Squeeze the juice from the oranges and lemons and put in a preserving pan or large saucepan with the shredded peel. Scrape the orange pulp from the skins. Roughly chop it and add to the pan. Roughly chop half the remaining skins and tie in a large square of muslin with the pips. Add to the pan with 2 litres (3½ pints) water and bring to the boil.

Reduce the heat and simmer gently, uncovered, for about 1½ hours until the shredded peel is very tender. Lift out the muslin bag from the pan, pressing it against the side to squeeze out as much juice as possible. Discard the bag.

Stir in the sugar and heat gently until dissolved. Bring to the boil and boil until setting point is reached, about 15 minutes.

Leave to stand for 15 minutes to allow the peel to settle, then ladle into sterilized jars. Cover and label.

orange, sultana and whisky marmalade

This is a rich, chunky marmalade, flavoured with plump sultanas, muscovado sugar and a generous glug of whisky. Although it has a warm, wintry characteristic it can equally well be made at any time of the year when supplies run low.

makes about 2 kg (4 lb 6 oz)   **preparation time** 25 mins
cooking time 1¾ hours

1 kg (2 lb 3 oz) oranges

Juice of 2 lemons

200 g (7 oz) sultanas

500 g (1 lb 2 oz) light muscovado sugar

1.1 kg (2 lb 7oz) preserving or granulated sugar

75 ml (3 fl oz) whisky

Using a sharp knife, cut away the thin layer of peel, but not the white pith, from the oranges. Shred the peel thinly or thickly, depending on personal preference.

Squeeze the juice from the oranges and lemons and put in a preserving pan or large saucepan with the shredded peel. Scrape the orange pulp from the skins. Roughly chop it and add to the pan. Roughly chop half the remaining skins and tie in a large square of muslin with the pips. Add to the pan with 1.5 litres (2½ pints) water and bring to the boil.

Reduce the heat and simmer gently, uncovered, for 1 hour. Add the sultanas and cook for a further 15–30 minutes or until the shredded peel is very tender. Lift out the muslin bag from the pan, pressing it against the side to squeeze out as much juice as possible. Discard the bag.

Stir in the sugar and heat gently until dissolved. Bring to the boil and boil until setting point is reached, about 15 minutes. Turn off the heat and stir in the whisky.

Leave to stand for 15 minutes to allow the peel to settle, then ladle into sterilized jars. Cover and label.

melon and grapefruit marmalade

Use any melons, winter or summer varieties, for this mellow marmalade providing they're sweet, ripe and delicious. It's soft set and lightly jellied so should suit anyone who likes the chunkiness of the fruit but not too many shreds.

makes 2 kg (4 lb 6 oz)   **preparation time** 20 mins

cooking time 1 hour 10 mins

2 grapefruit

1 unwaxed lemon

1 ripe melon

1 kg (2 lb 3 oz) preserving or granulated sugar

Chop the grapefruit and lemon into small pieces, discarding the stalk ends and any pips. Blend, in batches, in a food processor until finely chopped.

Put in a preserving pan or large saucepan with 1 litre (1¾ pints) water. Bring to the boil, cover with a lid and reduce the heat. Cook very gently for about 45 minutes until the pieces of fruit are very tender.

While cooking, halve and deseed the melon and cut away the skin. Chop the flesh into small dice and add to the pan. Cook for a further 5 minutes.

Stir in the sugar and heat gently until dissolved. Bring to the boil and boil until setting point is reached, about 20 minutes.

Ladle into sterilized jars, cover and label.

pink grapefruit marmalade

Grapefruit have a reputation for being bitter due to their thick, pithy skins, but they make a delicious marmalade, more delicate than orange but still tangy and refreshing. Yellow grapefruit can be used instead of the pink, if liked.

makes 1.5 kg (3 lb 5 oz)   **preparation time** 25 mins   **cooking time** 1¼ hours

3 pink grapefruit

2 lemons

1 kg (2 lb 3 oz) preserving or granulated sugar

Using a sharp knife, cut away a thin layer of peel, but not the white pith, from the grapefruit. Shred the peel finely, or alternatively chop it in the food processor.

Squeeze the juice from the grapefruit and lemons and put in a preserving pan or large saucepan with the shredded or chopped peel. Scrape the grapefruit pulp from the skins. Roughly chop it and add to the pan. Roughly chop half the remaining skins and tie in a large square of muslin with the pips. Add to the pan with 1 litre (1¾ pints) water and bring to the boil.

Reduce the heat, cover with a lid and simmer gently for about 1 hour until the shredded peel is very tender. Lift out the muslin bag from the pan, pressing it against the side to squeeze out as much juice as possible. Discard the bag.

Stir in the sugar and heat gently until dissolved. Bring to the boil and boil until setting point is reached, about 15 minutes.

Leave to stand for 15 minutes to allow the peel to settle, then ladle into sterilized jars. Cover and label.

pineapple cheese

Cooking pineapple to a thick purée intensifies its flavour and it goes so well with grilled or barbecued pork and most smoked fish, including pâtés and terrines. The chilli creates quite a heat but can easily be halved for a milder flavour.

makes about 700 g (1 lb 9 oz)   **preparation time** 15 mins
cooking time 55 mins

1 large, ripe, juicy pineapple
(about 1.5 kg/3 lb 5 oz)

Juice of 2 limes

10 cardamom pods

½ tsp crushed dried chillies

400 g (14 oz) granulated or
caster sugar

Trim the ends off the pineapple and cut away the skin. Cut out the core and roughly dice the flesh. Put the flesh in a large saucepan with the lime juice and 300 ml (½ pint) water.

Bring to the boil, reduce the heat and cover with a lid. Simmer gently for 30 minutes until the pineapple is tender. While cooking, crush the cardamom pods to release the seeds. Discard the pods and lightly crush the seeds.

Blend the pineapple and juices in a food processor until smooth. Return to the cleaned pan with the dried chillies, cardamom seeds and sugar.

Cook over a gentle heat until the sugar has dissolved, then cook for a further 20–25 minutes or until the mixture is very thick. A wooden spoon, drawn across the base of the pan should leave a clear line through the mixture.

Ladle into sterilized jars, cover and label.

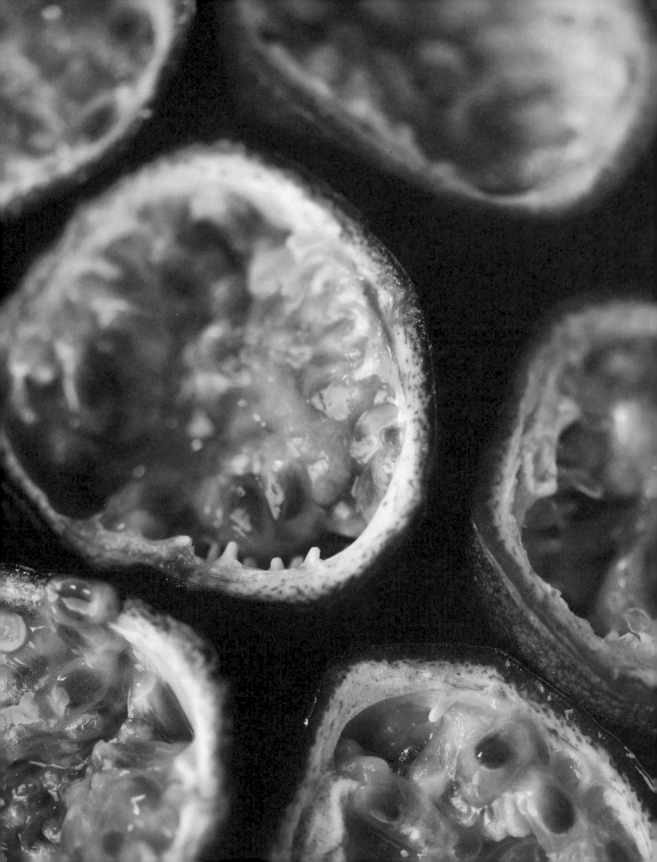

passionfruit curd

Passionfruit are at their ripest and sweetest when the skins are craggy and dimpled, perfect for giving this fruit curd plenty of juicy, tangy flavour. In this version, all the passionfruit pulp is used, but strain by pressing the pulp through a sieve to remove the seeds if you prefer. There's no need to increase the quantity of the fruit to compensate.

makes 700 g (1 lb 9 oz)   **preparation time** 10 mins   **cooking time** 25 mins

200 ml (7 fl oz) passionfruit pulp (about 10 fruits)

Juice of 1 lemon

250 g (9 oz) granulated or caster sugar

125 g (4½ oz) unsalted butter, cut into pieces

4 medium eggs

Put all the ingredients into a heatproof bowl that can rest over a saucepan of gently simmering water without the base of the bowl touching the water.

Position the bowl over the water and heat gently, whisking frequently until the butter has melted and the ingredients are smoothly combined.

Continue to stir the mixture over a gentle heat for about 15 minutes until it thickly coats the back of a wooden spoon.

Pour into sterilized jars, cover and label.

spiced cranberry and pear cheese

Serve this mildly spiced, tangy preserve with a creamy blue-veined cheese and crisp oatcakes for a simple lunchtime snack. It can also be set in little pots or small preserving jars to accompany the cheeseboard for winter entertaining.

makes approx 850 g (1 lb 14 oz)   **preparation time** 20 mins
cooking time 45 mins

500 g (1 lb 2 oz) ripe pears

500 g (1 lb 2 oz) cranberries

100 ml (3½ fl oz) cranberry juice

1 tbsp allspice berries

1 cinnamon stick

250 g (9 oz) granulated or caster sugar for every 500 g (1 lb) fruit purée

Roughly chop the pears. There's no need to peel or core them as the fruits will be strained after cooking.

Put the pears, cranberries, cranberry juice and spices in a large saucepan with 300 ml (½ pint) water. Bring to the boil, cover with a lid and reduce the heat. Cook gently for about 30 minutes until the fruits are soft and pulpy.

Press the mixture through a sieve, extracting as much pulp as possible with the back of a spoon. Measure the purée. Return to the cleaned pan and add the sugar.

Cook over a gentle heat until the sugar has dissolved, then cook for a further 15 minutes or until the mixture is very thick. A wooden spoon, drawn across the base of the pan should leave a clear line through the mixture.

Ladle into sterilized jars, cover and label.

sweet pickled cranberries

Pickling cranberries with sugar and vinegar makes a tangier alternative to the more familiar cranberry sauce for accompanying roast turkey. They also provide a sweet, tangy contrast to other rich meats, pork pies and pâtés.

makes 1.25 kg (2 lb 12 oz)   **preparation time** 10 mins   **cooking time** 10 mins

1 kg (2 lb 3 oz) cranberries

275 g (9½ oz) light muscovado sugar

250 ml (9 fl oz) red or white wine vinegar

50 ml (2 fl oz) port

2 cinnamon sticks

Pared rind of 2 oranges

Put the cranberries in a large saucepan with the sugar and vinegar. Heat gently until the cranberries starts to pop.

Stir in the port, cinnamon stick and orange rind and cook gently over a moderate heat until the cranberries have softened slightly.

Ladle into small, thoroughly clean jars. Cover and store in a cool place for up to 6 months.

hot mango chutney

Mango chutney is invariably served with curries, but its fruity, spicy flavour makes it as adaptable as any other chutney. Try it with chicken salads or sandwiches, baked ham, cold roast pork or even salty cheeses such as Halloumi. For a less fiery flavour reduce the chilli by half or more.

makes 1.6 kg (3½ lb)   **preparation time** 25 mins   **cooking time** 40 mins

2.4 kg (5¼ lb) ripe mangoes (about 5 large fruit)

2 onions, finely chopped

2 tsp crushed dried chillies

3 garlic cloves, crushed

75 g (3 oz) fresh root ginger, grated

2 tsp garam masala

½ tsp salt

400 ml (14 fl oz) distilled malt vinegar

325 g (11½ oz) granulated sugar

Slice the mangoes, either side of the flat stone. Roughly chop all the flesh, discarding the stones and skins.

Put all the ingredients in a preserving pan or large saucepan and heat until the sugar dissolves. Bring to the boil. Reduce the heat and simmer gently, uncovered, for 35–40 minutes until the mango is very tender and translucent, and the juices are thick. If the mangoes remain in chunky pieces, break them down a bit with a potato masher, but take care as the mixture will be very hot.

Ladle into thoroughly clean jars, cover and label.

mostarda

Mostarda is an Italian preserve for which there are so many different recipes and variations. Some are thick smooth purées, others fruits suspended in syrup, but all contain one vital ingredient – mustard. This version, made using a mixture of dried fruits can accompany cold meat or, less traditionally, served with lightly sweetened ricotta, mascarpone or cream cheese.

makes 900 g (2 lb)   **preparation time** 15 mins   **cooking time** 20 mins

1 lemon

1 litre (1¾ pints) white grape juice

500 g (1 lb 2 oz) mixture of dried fruits, such as prunes, figs, dates and apricots, roughly chopped

100 g (3½ oz) clear honey

2 tbsp mustard powder

Squeeze the juice from the lemon. Halve the lemon skins and cut away the pith and membrane. Dice the peel and put in a saucepan with the grape juice. Bring to the boil and cook for 5–10 minutes until the juice is reduced by about a third.

Add the dried fruits, lemon juice and honey to the pan and sprinkle in the mustard. Cook gently, uncovered until the fruits have plumped up and most of the juices have been absorbed.

Ladle into sterilized jars, cover and label.

indian lime pickle

Although these limes are preserved in oil, they're known as a pickle because of their spicy, sour flavour that becomes more mellow during storage. Lime pickles are made for Indian dishes but are also good with cold meats and 'meaty' fish such as tuna.

makes 750 g (1 lb 10 oz)   **preparation time** 20 mins, plus brining

cooking time 2 mins

7 small limes, preferably unwaxed

75 g (3 oz) salt

1 tsp crushed dried chillies

1 tbsp black mustard seeds, crushed

1 tbsp cumin seeds, crushed

1 tbsp fenugreek seeds, crushed

1 tsp ground turmeric

Approx 300 ml (½ pint) mild olive oil, or a mixture of olive and vegetable oil

Cut each lime lengthways into 8 wedges. Toss with the salt in a bowl. Cover and leave to stand for 3 days, turning the limes daily.

Rinse off the salt and pat dry on kitchen paper. Pack into thoroughly clean, wide-necked preserving jars with a total capacity of 750 ml (1¼ pints).

Put the chillies, mustard seeds, cumin and fenugreek seeds in a frying pan and dry-fry for 2 minutes. Lightly grind the spices using a pestle and mortar, food processor or spice grinder. Turn into a jug and add the turmeric and oil.

Stir well and pour over the limes until covered. (Add a little more oil if necessary to top up the jars.) Cover and store in a cool place for 2 weeks before using. Unopened jars will keep for up to 6 months.

hazelnuts in caramel

This nut-infused sauce makes a fabulous topping for ice cream, yogurt and creamy desserts, as well as for pancakes, drop scones and baked bananas. It can be served straight from the jar, or warmed through gently in a small saucepan with a splash of cream.

makes 350 g (12½ oz)   **preparation time** 10 mins   **cooking time** 15 mins

150 g (5½ oz) blanched hazelnuts

150 g (5½ oz) caster sugar

Finely grated zest of 1 orange, plus 3 tbsp juice

1 tbsp Cointreau or other orange-flavoured liqueur (optional)

Scatter the hazelnuts on a foil-lined grill rack and grill until lightly toasted. Lightly chop so the hazelnuts are still in chunky pieces.

Half fill a small bowl (or the washing up bowl) with cold water. Heat the sugar in a small saucepan with 150 ml (¼ pint) water until the sugar dissolves. Bring to the boil and cook for 5–10 minutes until the syrup has turned to a golden caramel. Immediately remove from the heat and immerse the base of the pan in the water to prevent further cooking, taking care as the pan will splutter.

Add the orange zest and juice to the pan with 4 tablespoons water and return to the heat, stirring until the hardened caramel has softened to make a smooth sauce. Stir in the liqueur, if using, and hazelnuts and remove from the heat.

Turn into 2 x 150 ml (¼ pint) sterilized jars and cover with screw-topped lids. Store for up to 6 months.

pecans in maple syrup

Simply steeping pecan nuts in maple syrup mingles the flavours together, making a lovely topping for vanilla ice cream or for spooning over yogurt, warm sponge puddings, cheesecakes and other creamy desserts.

makes 600 g (1 lb 5 oz)   **preparation time** 5 mins   **cooking time** 2 mins

250 g (9 oz) shelled pecan nuts, very roughly chopped

400 ml (14 fl oz) maple syrup

2 cinnamon sticks

Scatter the chopped nuts on a foil-lined grill rack and grill until lightly toasted.

Pack the nuts into 2 sterilized 300 ml (½ pint) jars, add a cinnamon stick to each jar.

Heat the maple syrup in a small saucepan until hot but not boiling and pour over the nuts, tapping the jar on the surface to release any air bubbles. Cover with a screw-topped lid and store in a cool place for up to 6 months.

VARIATION For honeyed walnuts, use the same quantities. Sprigs of bruised thyme leaves can be tucked into the jar instead of the cinnamon stick.

marsala steeped raisins

When dried fruit is steeped in alcohol for some time it plumps up, absorbing the flavour and at the same time turning the alcohol slightly syrupy with its sweetness. Use the soft juicy raisins in cakes, puddings and desserts as you'd use regular dried ones. The Marsala can be used to add a sweet kick to pan sauces, custards and creamy desserts. Alternatively, spoon both fruit and juices over ice cream, creamy rice pudding, baked apples or bananas, warm custard or almond tarts.

makes 300 g (10½ oz)   **preparation time** 2 mins

200 g (7 oz) raisins

200 ml (7 fl oz) Marsala or sherry

Put the raisins in a thoroughly clean screw-topped jar and add the Marsala or sherry.

Screw on the lid and store for a week before using, shaking the jar occasionally. Store for up to 6 months.

VARIATION Use equal quantities of any of the following combinations: dried cranberries in orange liqueur, dried figs or prunes in Armagnac or brandy, dried apricots in Disaronno (or other almond liqueur), dried blueberries in vanilla vodka.

almond and amaretti mincemeat

If you like almonds this recipe is a real must. Although it contains crushed almond biscuits, the liqueur prevents it deteriorating too quickly. Store in a cool, dry place for up to six months, checking occasionally for deterioration.

makes 900 g (2 lb)   **preparation time** 15 mins, plus standing

125 g (4½ oz) blanched almonds, chopped

100 g (3½ oz) no-soak dried apricots, chopped

100 g (4 oz) raisins

100 g (4 oz) sultanas

50 g (2 oz) currants

½ tsp ground cinnamon

¼ tsp ground nutmeg

100 ml (3½ fl oz) Disaronno liqueur or brandy

Finely grated zest and juice of 1 orange

75 g (3 oz) light muscovado sugar

75 g (3 oz) amaretti biscuits

1 cooking apple (about 250 g/9 oz)

Mix together the almonds, apricots, raisins, sultanas, currants, spices, liqueur, orange zest and juice and sugar in a large bowl. Crumble the amaretti biscuits over the ingredients and stir in.

Peel the apple and grate the flesh into the bowl, working around the core. Mix into the other ingredients. Cover with cling film and leave to stand for several hours to let the flavours mingle.

Stir well and pack the mincemeat into sterilized jars, pressing down firmly with the back of a spoon to eliminate all the air bubbles. Spoon over any syrupy juices left in the bowl. Cover and label.

sloe gin

Sloes are very small, wild plums, the fruit of the blackthorn tree. Ripe and ready for picking in late autumn, this delicious liqueur will be just about ready in time to serve as a treat on cold winter days. Left for longer the flavour will mature, mellow and improve. Damsons can be used in exactly the same way.

makes 900 ml (1½ pints) **preparation time** 10 mins, plus standing

450 g (1 lb) sloes
125 g (4½ oz) caster sugar
750 ml (1¼ pint) gin

Discard the stalks from the sloes. Wash them and prick all over with a fine skewer. Put in a large, thoroughly clean screw-topped jar with the sugar and gin.

Secure the lid and shake the jar several times. Leave for a week, shaking the jar occasionally to dissolve the sugar.

Store in a cool place for at least 3 months. Strain through a muslin-lined sieve into a jug. Pour into thoroughly clean clip or screw-topped bottles.

cranberry and apple mincemeat

Cranberries are lovely in this mincemeat, adding a bright colour and fresh, tangy flavour. It should appeal to those who find bought mincemeat too sweet. Stored in a cool place, it will keep for up to three months.

makes 2 kg (4 lb 6 oz) **preparation time** 15 mins, plus standing

500 g (1 lb 2 oz) cooking apples
Finely grated zest and juice of 2 unwaxed lemons
375 g (13 oz) cranberries
50 g (2 oz) stem ginger from a jar, finely chopped
650 g (1 lb 7 oz) mixed dried fruit
50 g (2 oz) chopped mixed peel
325 g (11½ oz) light muscovado sugar
200 g (7 oz) beef or vegetable suet
1 tsp ground mixed spice
100 ml (3½ fl oz) brandy

Peel the apples and grate the flesh into a large bowl, working around the core. Stir in the lemon zest and juice. The lemon will stop the apples browning.

Roughly chop the cranberries. This is easiest done in the food processor, but don't overblend, they need to remain in large pieces. Add the cranberries to the bowl with the remaining ingredients. Mix well and cover the bowl with cling film. Leave to stand for several hours to let the flavours mingle.

Stir well and pack the mincemeat into sterilized jars, pressing down firmly with the back of a spoon to eliminate all the air bubbles. Spoon over any syrupy juices left in the bowl. Cover and label.

clementines in brandied caramel

This is the preserved answer to 'oranges in caramel'. It's equally delicious, definitely more alcoholic and ready and waiting whenever you fancy a treat. Serve with melting vanilla ice cream or pouring cream.

makes 1 litre (1¾ pints)   **preparation time** 20 mins   **cooking time** 30 mins

10 clementines

175 g (6 oz) caster sugar

Pared zest of 1 lemon, plus the squeezed juice

3 bay leaves

300 ml (½ pint) Grand Marnier or other orange-flavoured liqueur

Carefully peel the clementines, leaving the fruits whole, and remove any pith from the fruits. Prick the clementines all over with a skewer so they'll be able to absorb the syrup.

Half fill a large bowl or the washing up bowl with cold water. Put the sugar in a small, heavy-based saucepan with 150 ml (¼ pint) water and heat gently until the sugar has dissolved. Bring to the boil and boil until the syrup turns to a golden caramel. Watch the syrup closely as it cooks. Once it's golden, it'll very quickly overcook and turn bitter. Immerse the base of the pan in the bowl of water to prevent further cooking.

Stir in another 150 ml (¼ pint) water and return to the heat. Add the lemon zest and juice and bay leaves and heat gently until the caramel has melted and the syrup is smooth.

Pour the syrup into a larger saucepan and add the clementines and liqueur. Cook gently for 15 minutes.

Spoon the fruits into a 1 litre (1¾ pint) or two 500 ml (18 fl oz) sterilized, wide-necked preserving jars. Pour the syrup, including the bay and pared lemon, over the top so the clementines are covered. Cover with lids and leave to cool. Store in a cool place, or refrigerate for up to 2 months.

figs in spiced syrup

This recipe preserves fresh figs in a spice-infused syrup that's perfect for an after-dinner treat with strong coffee. It makes one jar but you can easily double up on quantities if you find a reasonably priced supply. It's even good for over-ripe figs that might be a little soft for eating raw.

makes 500 ml (18 fl oz) **preparation time** 10 mins
cooking time 5 mins, plus sterilizing

7 small figs, halved
75 g (3 oz) granulated sugar
½ tsp ground mixed spice
2 tbsp lemon juice
4 tbsp brandy or rum

Preheat the oven to 150°C/300°F/Gas Mark 2. Pack the figs into a sterilized 500 ml (18 fl oz) wide-necked preserving jar.

Put the sugar in a saucepan with the spice and 300 ml (½ pint) water. Heat gently until the sugar dissolves. Bring to the boil and boil for 5 minutes. Stir in the lemon juice, then the brandy or rum.

Pour the syrup over the figs so they're completely covered and tap the jar on the surface to release any air bubbles. Push a thin-bladed knife or skewer down the sides of the jar to release any bubbles you can see through the glass.

Position the lids and rubber seals if using but don't tighten the lids. Place the jar in a newspaper-lined roasting tin. Cook for 30 minutes. Remove from the oven and immediately seal the jar. Label and store for up to 6 months.

index

picture credits

iStockphotos.com
Pages 19, 20, 24, 28, 30, 32, 34, 38, 42, 44, 47, 52, 56, 57, 61, 62, 65, 68, 70, 72, 74, 76, 78, 80, 81, 83, 84, 88, 90, 92, 94, 96, 98, 101, 102, 104, 106, 108, 110, 112, 114, 116, 118, 120, 125, 126, 128, 130, 134, 136, 138, 140, 141, 142, 144, 146, 148, 150, 152, 156
Stockfood Ltd
Front cover image